SUBTLE DIFFERENCES, BIG FAUX PAS
TEST YOUR CULTURAL COMPETENCE

Elizabeth Vennekens-Kelly

First Published Great Britain 2012, Second edition published 2013 by Summertime Publishing

© Copyright Elizabeth Vennekens-Kelly

All rights reserved. No part of this publication may be reproduced, stored in or introduced into a retrieval system, or transmitted, in any form, or by any means (electronic, mechanical, photocopying recording or otherwise) without the prior written permission of the publisher.

This book is sold subject to the condition that it shall not, by way of trade or otherwise, be lent, resold, hired out, or otherwise circulated without the publisher's prior consent in any form of binding or cover other than that in which it is published and without a similar condition including this condition being imposed on the subsequent purchaser.

Der Grüne Punkt – Duales System Deutschland GmbH holds the rights to the trademark "Der Grüne Punkt"

"Stick people" created by A Bit Better Corp. Microsoft holds copyright permission for images used in this book and taken from Microsoft Office 2012 Desktop Application Software. Terms can be found in section 3c of its License Terms.

GINETEX laundry symbols used with permission.

ISBN: 978-1-904881-66-7

Design by Creationbooth.com

DISCLAIMER

Some names have been changed to protect identities.

To my husband, Paul, who introduced me to his world and all its wonders.

I love my life and it's better because of you.

ACKNOWLEDGMENTS

This book would not have come to fruition without the support and eagle eyes of Jill Goldsmith and Amy Bohanon. I will forever be indebted to Constance Anderson who suggested I put my ideas on paper. Andrea Martins, entrepreneur and author of *Expat Women: Confessions,* was an inspiration. She guided me to Jo Parfitt at Summertime Publishing. Jo has been the source of valuable insight and information and pulled me through when I did not believe I would finish the task at hand.

I want to acknowledge the diverse and interesting people with whom I have worked, taught and had the pleasure of meeting in the last eleven years. They introduced me to their world and were an integral part of a new phase in my life, for which I will forever be grateful. Specifically Brigitta and Robert Wellendorf-Werner, who befriended and welcomed us to Germany, the fascinating folks I met through Berlitz in Offenbach, Germany and in Antwerp, Belgium, Greet Verellen, who followed my advice and wowed them in New York, Stephan Statijn of NDL/HIDC who liked my message and gave me an opportunity to share it with an international audience. Luciana Fava and Diana Smith Walsh, who worked with me on the FAWCO Sharing Cultures task force. I want to thank all the people who deliberately or unwittingly contributed to the content.

Thank you to my family and friends who listened to my stories and encouraged me to share them with others.

Last, but not least I want to thank my amazing husband, Paul, whose love, kindness and patience give me the strength to do anything.

TABLE OF CONTENTS

Introduction 1

Language and Communication 9
The Power of a Few Words 10
Speaking the Local Language - Why Bother? 14
English is English 20
What's the Weather Like Back Home 26
Getting the Message Right 32
Thumbs Up 38
Oh, Those Colorful Words We Learn 44
Did You Hear The One About? 50

Business Practices and Communication 55
May I Have your Card, Please? 56
May I Call You Steve? 60
Round the Clock 66
Substance vs Style 70
One Size Fits All 74
Where to Draw the Line 80
Are You Hiring? 84
Accompanying Partner or Trailing Spouse 90

Everyday Living 97
Do the Numbers Add Up? 98
The Devil's in the Details 104
May I Help You? 110
Domestic Goddess 116
But It Was On Television 122

Lifestyles, Attitudes and Tradition 129
One Stop Shopping 130
The Grammar of Food 136
It's A Celebration 142
Polite or Rude? That is the Question 146
Cheers! 152
Babies, Weddings and Funerals 156
Hats Off to You 162
Naked or Nude? 168
Luck of the Irish 174
Man's Best Friend 178
This Is So Taxing 184
Separation of Church and State 190

Conclusion 197
Quiz Answers..199
Resources 225
About the Author 231

INTRODUCTION

Whet your Appetite

Some people and cultures have perfected the art of subtleties and are able to communicate their desires with a single gesture. Then there are those, who, even if hit over the head by a two by four, miss the message.

Edward T. Hall, the father of intercultural relations, who developed the concept of 'high' and 'low' context communication, explained that cultures and people do not convey their messages in the same way. The 'high context' crowd use suggestions and indirect approaches to express their thoughts, while 'low context' cultures and individuals tell you exactly what they think. US citizens, although not the most extreme 'low context' group, are certainly one of the front runners. Subtlety or ambiguity rarely work, consider:

> My parents decided to call me by the nickname, Beth, instead of my given name. However, when I relocated to Europe I opted to use my given name, Elizabeth. For years I have signed emails, card and letters, Elizabeth, and yet replies always start 'Dear Beth.' I recently included in an email to a very good friend the question, "Would you mind calling me Elizabeth?" Her mortified answer was, "I had no idea you wanted to be called Elizabeth. Of course, I'll call you this." I had to laugh because she had never gotten my indirect request. Although friends and family would tell you they know exactly what I am thinking, I have tried to tone down my communication style using more hints. I'm not convinced this method works!

Some people, countries and cultures are quite isolated, meaning their exposure to cultural variations is limited. The result is they may not realize there are differences, or other acceptable ways of communicating, eating, living or conducting business.

For some, 'different' is exciting or fascinating, but many people view things they consider to be 'unconventional' with trepidation. They consider 'non-traditional' to be frightening or intimidating and see these things in a negative light. When you interact with people from cultures other than your own it is helpful for you to look beyond outward appearances.

> If you saw a Dutchman wearing wooden clogs you would think they were uncomfortable and outdated, in fact they are very practical for walking through wet, muddy, fields.

When people speak the same language, have similar attire and generally look like us, the assumption is made that they must have comparable values, attitudes and beliefs. While this certainly could be true, the external can be misleading. All too often we presume any differences are minor and inconsequential. When a US American business person is relocating or beginning to work with someone from the United Kingdom he/she may think, 'same language, no big deal'. However, as Toni Summers Hargis, author of *Rules, Britannia – an Insider's Guide to Life in the United Kingdom,* exemplifies, it is not that straightforward. The American may not need language lessons to speak and write the language, but he or she may benefit from understanding the nuances of British English and by doing so will gain respect from the people around him/her. Cultural enlightenment is crucial. The US citizen needs preparation for the UK just as much as understanding the customs and traditions of Senegal will help the Italian and his family, who accept an assignment in West Africa.

There are fantastic resources available to the person who wants to read comprehensively on cultural differences. Books written by Edward T. Hall, Richard Lewis, and Terri Morrison and Wayne A. Conaway such as *The Hidden Dimension, When Cultures Collide,* and *Kiss, Bow, or*

Shake Hands are terrific. These books provide in-depth information about cultural differences and country-specific information. In addition to the volume of quality material published on the value of cultural awareness or intelligence, there are well-known examples of business setbacks, where culture clash was a factor in an embarrassing faux pas. A representative for Associates for International Research, Inc. (AIRINC) stated that most expatriates come from:

- USA
- UK
- India
- Germany
- France
- China
- Canada
- Australia
- Singapore
- Hong Kong

If you are part of the 'globally mobile', understanding cultural differences is not only interesting but essential. Gaining an understanding of other nations' cultural similarities and contradictions can be fun and rewarding.

My cross-cultural journey

There are many factors influencing how we think and react to new and different situations, including family, culture, geographic region, religion and experiences. In our family, we were raised by broad-minded parents, who taught us to see everyone as equal regardless of race, color, creed, religion, or gender. When we moved to New Mexico in the southwestern part of the United States, we met individuals with cultural backgrounds that were new to me including, Hispanics and Native Americans. I was introduced to new customs and traditions; hosting a *Quinceañera* party for 15-year-old Hispanic girls, and learning the Navajo language is a spoken not written one. This was my introduction to the concept that cultural differences are fascinating, things are done differently but cultural variations are not 'wrong.'

Several exchange students attended our high school and I suggested our family host a student. The family was open to the idea, although my brother expressed concerns about hosting someone from an Asian country; he worried about the cultural differences. Despite these concerns, the guidance counselor recommended we open our home to a Japanese girl. Without any training or guidance, on either side of the Pacific, the decision was made that Nahoko, a 15-year-old girl, would live with our family for a year. How naïve we were.

We knew nothing about the importance of saving face. Sometimes Nahoko would say, "Yes" rather than be a burden and ask for clarification of something she didn't understand. Although her English reading and writing skills were exceptional; they were the focus of the Japanese school system, understanding when someone spoke or being able to express herself were much more difficult. Sometimes she would nod, and we would interpret the gesture as being that she understood, which was not always the case. We lived in a suburb and getting together with her school friends meant asking for a ride from my parents or us, and she did not want to be a bother. My brothers and I continued to lead our hectic teenage-lives with little thought of including Nahoko.

By Christmas it was evident that unless she was playing the piano, she was unhappy. We didn't know how to modify our lifestyle so it was decided Nahoko would move in with another family to finish the school year. This was my first experience of living alongside someone from another culture and it failed miserably. Hindsight is always 20/20 and now I know I would do things very differently.

I wish I had tried to learn more than three words of Japanese, had inquired about her country and the way things are done and why. I missed out on an amazing opportunity. Although we lost contact for many years, Nahoko recently found me and we have reconnected. Slowly she is teaching me about the Japanese culture.

Meeting my Belgian husband, Paul, in 1999 was the beginning of a new phase of my life. We moved from Phoenix, Arizona USA to Europe, where I was introduced to people from all over the world with whom I would have to communicate, make friends and do business.

Some of them spoke my language but had a strong accent or used English words I had never heard before such as 'pram' and 'lorry'. I met dual-culture couples and expat women who spoke English and dressed as I did, but we had different attitudes toward education, work, marriage, money and more. On the surface we might have seemed alike, but frequently we reacted to situations in different ways. For example, punctuality was important to me, but not to Justine from Ireland, who thought nothing of arriving 15-20 minutes late for the lessons she was giving. And David, a Canadian, spoke rudimentary German with the locals, while I hesitated because my German wasn't perfect.

There were other non-Europeans who dressed differently, spoke Portuguese, Persian and Arabic dialects, some followed another religion or an entirely different way of life. Yet these people lived in my street, shopped in the same shops and attended the same social events.

Sometimes the differences between people, their experiences and expectations, are vast, while other times there are so many similarities the differences are minuscule. It is important to ask questions, to learn from, and not make assumptions about people from another culture. One of my classmates in my German course was from Afghanistan. The US was at war with the Taliban in her country so I hesitated to interact with her, or to tell her my nationality, because I feared she would see me as 'the enemy.' She did not; she saw me as someone like herself, a newlywed, an immigrant and someone trying to make a new start in a foreign country.

Friends and family thought I was living a fairytale life, not because I was a princess, but because I was having the opportunity to visit places around the world, try new things and meet people from other lands. They were right, this was the start of my journey into intercultural awareness.

Because my brothers and I were raised not to see the differences in people, there was a tendency on my part to ignore the variations. I was uneasy acknowledging that someone was from a different ethnic group, or that I did not understand someone's desire to remain on the tribal reservation, because it would mean I must be prejudiced. In retrospect this attitude helped me to be non-judgmental, but it may have not encouraged me to see the whole picture. I know now there are similarities and differences between people, whether they look the same and act the same, look the same but act different, look different but act the same or look different and act different.

In the mobile world in which we live it has never been so important to acknowledge, learn about and then embrace the variations among the people who share our planet. One of the goals of this book is to encourage you to research cultures in which you are interested. My own research led me to new discoveries, such as the sensitivity around the use of the term 'Americans' exclusively by US citizens. This will be addressed in more detail later, but you will see I have opted to use the US Americans instead of Americans. As you learn more about the cultures of people with whom you are living and working it will reduce cultural myths and fallacies.

20 common myths and fallacies

1. Wearing Western style clothes automatically means its wearers have similar thoughts and beliefs as those from Western cultures
2. Donning traditional garments, such as headscarves, kilts, means its wearers are old-fashioned and not forward thinking
3. Being on time is a sign of respect
4. Not speaking the local language means someone is unintelligent and/or uninterested in integrating
5. English is English. If you speak it everyone will understand you perfectly
6. A dog is man's best friend
7. Everyone uses 8.5 inch by 11inch paper
8. Blu-ray discs and DVDs are interchangeable and can be operated in any machine around the world
9. Burping in public is rude
10. What you know is always more important than who you know.
11. Calling someone by their first name is friendly and a good way to develop a working relationship
12. The customer is always right

13. Giving someone the 'thumbs-up' is always a positive gesture
14. Black should be worn to a funeral
15. If someone is born in a country he or she is automatically a citizen of that country
16. Family is a neutral small talk topic
17. Humor is a great tool in business
18. Shaking hands is always a good way to greet someone
19. Jan is a girl's name
20. Everyone lives to work

Cultural misunderstandings can occur about many things that you do, or think, or say automatically. Not so. The list below shares some examples of things you might **NOT** expect to be regulated in your host country, but may be:

1. Where you can wash your car
2. What you can name your dog
3. Opening hours of business
4. Retail sales periods
5. Showing public affection
6. How you dress
7. Making comments about the Holocaust
8. The color of your trash bags
9. Where livestock can be housed and/or wander
10. Who inherits your money

That is why I wrote this book. To raise your awareness of the issues I see now, but did not see when we invited Nahoko to live with us for a year.

In our personal lives mistakes are embarrassing, but in business they can be costly. Many of the issues and challenges I have experienced, or learned about through my work, are presented in the following pages.

This book is a series of snippets on topics. Each section is followed by a short, fun quiz where more than one answer could be right. It is not an exhaustive list, but the goal is to pique your interest and give you an appetite for more. This book is not big. It is a cultural primer, if you will, your first step towards appreciating and understanding the global world and its wonderful people. I hope the material will make you smile while raising your awareness and highlight some of the cultural faux pas waiting to trip you up.

I have lived in Europe, dividing my time between Belgium and Germany, since 2001. I have worked or made friends with people from more than 40 countries and I am invited to give intercultural training to businesses and organizations. I have worked with companies like Sony - and presented on these issues at international conferences, for instance Families in Global Transition (FIGT) and the Federation of American Women's Clubs Overseas (FAWCO).

I hope this book will eliminate some of the myths and fallacies of various cultures and ensure you are better prepared for cross-cultural experiences.

This is your first step towards intercultural competence. I hope you enjoy the journey and have some fun at the same time.

Elizabeth Vennekens-Kelly

www.crossculture-training.be

Business English and Cross Cultural Consulting
Director

Steenschuitlaan 12
2830 Tisselt
BELGIUM
+32 474 211 912
e.kelly@crossculture-training.be

LANGUAGE AND COMMUNICATION

The Power of a Few Words

Not everyone is expected to be a linguist, but knowing a few elementary words can make a positive impression on the new people you will meet and greet as you travel around the world. Although English is spoken by more and more people, an effort made to speak the local language is appreciated.

Opens doors

A few basic words are commonly used during initial conversations. Being acquainted with these words in the language of your host country improves your image and is appreciated by the residents. Native speakers are usually more interested in helping someone who has made an attempt to speak their language.

> During a recent trip to Portugal, my husband and I entered a beautiful government building and were tentatively looking around, we didn't know whether we were allowed in the building or not. We saw a stern government official and assumed we would have to leave, but I said *"Bom Dia,"* 'good morning' and smiled. The gentleman indicated we were welcome to look around and take pictures. A bit of effort at making simple pleasantries goes a long way.

Beyond the door

Learning to ask a few basic questions can be helpful, such as:
- How much…?
- Where is…?
- May I…?
- Could you…?

> **WATCH OUT!**
> **Remember that understanding the answer may be a challenge, so pay attention.**

Being able to ask if someone speaks your language or whether they mind if you speak it in the language of the local country is invaluable. Make sure you learn to say:

- Do you speak...?
- May I speak..?

Ensure you can at least buy yourself a sandwich and a bottle of water in the foreign language and that you recognize the names for essential supermarket items. Pointing and miming are always helpful, but speaking a few words will endear you to your host culture.

> One of the first conferences Peggy attended in Nice, France, she noticed small flags on some of the name tags. She thought they were colorful and wondered why only a select group got to have the interesting name badges. It turned out the flags denoted the languages the individual conference representatives spoke.

International conferences and some hotels use flags to designate who can help visitors in a common language. Look out for them.

> **TIP**
> **When you say *'Good Morning'*, *'Buenas Dias'*, *'Goedemorgen'*, *'Ni hao'*, *'Buongiorno'* or *'Ohio Gezimus'* the world gets a little brighter.**

QUIZ – THE POWER OF A FEW WORDS

1. Match the greeting with the country:

Greeting	Country
Goedemorgen	Portugal
Bom Dia	Hungary
Bonjour	China
Jó reggelt	France
Ni hao	The Netherlands

2. In all of these countries except one, the nodding of the head up and down signifies, 'No', which one?

   a. Albania
   b. Bulgaria
   c. Sri Lanka
   d. Spain

3. In which country does 'how are you?' have the same meaning as 'hello' or 'good morning' because it is a rhetorical question to which a genuine reply is not expected?

   a. Finland
   b. Russia
   c. Ghana
   d. United States
   e. Argentina

4. In which country is it common for people to say 'good morning' and 'goodbye' when entering and exiting elevators in hotels, office buildings, and so on?

   a. Denmark
   b. Germany
   c. Indonesia
   d. Canada
   e. Somalia

5. Smiling, making eye contact with strangers, for example, when walking down the street is interpreted as friendly in every country.

   a. True
   b. False

Speak the Local Language – Why Bother?

When people immigrate or relocate to another country frequently they do not speak the local language. Some of the reasons given for not learning it include:

- No time
- It is a temporary assignment
- They can get by with English
- The language courses are too expensive
- They have a relative to help them with translations
- The local language is too obscure, they won't use it anywhere else

Universal excuse

Norwegian, Congolese and Hungarian are languages primarily spoken in one country and consequently they are often unpopular to learn.

> Businessmen from Angola, S. Korea and Israel, who studied English in Antwerp, explained they were taking English lessons instead of Dutch because Dutch had such limited application.

John Mole, author of *Mind Your Manners*, outlines several benefits of speaking and having an understanding of a local tongue, beyond the obvious of being better able to make yourself understood:

- Provides insight into how the other culture thinks
- Shows respect and courtesy

Grammar

Grammar rules are not the same in every language. English does not distinguish between formal and informal use of the 'you' form when conjugating its verbs, although German and French do. Chinese has only one tense and Finnish does not differentiate between feminine and masculine genders for their nouns. When you are new to a language it is easy to find yourself inadvertently using the grammatical rules of your mother tongue in the new language. Speaking another language requires determination, motivation, application and some considerable cost. Local residents are aware of this and welcome the effort of those who have taken the time to learn their language. If you have ever reached fluency in another language you will know how long it takes and will appreciate the effort taken by those learning yours.

Courtesy

The advantages of speaking a local language always outweigh not being able to communicate with residents, business associates, and so on. Doing so demonstrates respect, politeness and worthiness. Speaking the local language is not without its challenges.

> The German saying *"Da hast du aber Schwein gehabt!"* loosely translated means, 'you have been lucky enough to…' When Thomas, a US businessman, was asked if he had met Mr. Werner's wife, Thomas said in his best German, *"Nein, dieses Schwein habe ich noch nicht gehabt."* Thomas had modified the saying for the situation, but like many idioms they can only be used in one specific way or it changes the meaning. In this case Thomas called his boss' wife 'a pig' and implied that he had not yet had sex with her, yet. Subtle difference, big faux pas.

There may be times when a non-native speaker is dealing with a critical situation and prefers to use their own language in order to ensure they are understood, but in general you will always benefit from learning your host language.

TIP
Try not to consider English as the easy way out. Be a role model to other newcomers and learn the local language.

Local response

When foreigners attempt to speak with the local citizens and the locals respond in English it is easy to interpret this action as arrogance. The non-native speakers wonder whether they made a mistake or their accent was hard to understand. Sometimes though, their effort is rewarded with a smile and a positive answer spoken slowly and clearly in the local language. However the example below is typical in Belgium:

> **Customer:** *Geodemorgen, ik wil graag een kopje thee, alstublieft.* (May I have a cup of tea, please?)
>
> **Waiter:** Would you like milk or lemon with your tea?
>
> **Customer:** *Gewoon thee en een stuk gebak, alstublieft.* (Without milk, and a piece of cake, please.)
>
> **Waiter:** Okay, regular tea and a piece of cake, anything else.
>
> **Customer:** *Nee, dank U.* (No, thanks.)

In this example, the native English speaker is sitting in a café in Belgium and she wants to use her Flemish (a variation of Dutch) but the waiter hears her accent and responds in English. The customer believes her effort to speak the local language is being respectful of the country and wants to convey a recognition of the importance of the culture and customs. The waiter and his boss believe speaking to a customer in their native tongue is polite and helpful, and represents good customer service. It seems you can't win! If this were to happen to you, would you think the waiter was being courteous or condescending (because he thinks his English is better than your Flemish)?

TIP
**Encourage foreigners to use your local language –
don't perpetuate ignorance.**

QUIZ – SPEAK THE LOCAL LANGUAGE – WHY BOTHER?

1. A study commissioned by the European Union published in 2006 found businesses reported losing business or contracts due to:
   a. Lack of language skills
   b. Lack of cultural knowledge
   c. Not enough skilled labor
   d. Too much competition from China and India
   e. Both a lack of local language skills and cultural knowledge.

2. What is probably the most effective way of learning a foreign language and retaining the knowledge?
   a. a language course
   b. practice
   c. time
   d. a good teacher
   e. a grammar book and dictionary

3. Which of the following is not a learning style?
   a. Repetitive
   b. Visual
   c. Auditory
   d. Kinesthetic

4. Match the idiosyncrasy with the language

Idiosyncrasy	Language
Capitalizes all nouns	Finnish
No tenses	German
No gender	French
False friends	Chinese

5. Which country has a language requirement for its immigrants?

    a. Germany
    b. Canada
    c. France
    d. New Zealand
    e. All of the above

6. Which is not a language school?
    a. Berlitz Corporation
    b. Inlingua®
    c. Wall Street Institute
    d. Rosetta Stone
    e. Kid Castle Educational Corporation

7. Synonyms can have a positive or negative twist; put the words below in the right category.

Arrogant • Assured • Big-headed • Boastful • Cocky • Compliant   Conceited • Condescending • Distinguished • Docile • Egotistical • Full of oneself • Haughty • Imposing • Insecure • Meek   Mild • Modest • Plain • Pompous • Pretentious • Proud • Regal • Respectful • Retiring • Self-assured • Self-effacing • Self-important • Self-reliant • Self-sufficient • Simple • Stately • Submissive • Subservient • Sure of yourself • Timid • Unassuming • Unpretentious • Without airs

Confident		Humble	
Positive	**Negative**	**Positive**	**Negative**

English is English

It is said that the British and Americans are 'divided by a common language'. Let's look at the reality of that phrase more closely.

"Do you speak American?" The first time someone asked me I was stunned and wondered how well-informed the person was, then I discovered the variations in English are much more than a 'cool' accent or a few words such as 'loo' or 'mate'.

While French was the language of aristocrats and treated as a neutral vernacular when leaders needed a common communication platform, from the 18th to the middle of the 20th century, it is no longer the standard. English has transitioned into the primary language of business and beyond. Having one shared language can ease conversing challenges, but is English always English?

In the film *My Fair Lady*, Professor Higgins talks about the way English is spoken around the world. He says, "The Scotch and the Irish leave you close to tears... There are even places where English completely disappears. Why, in America they haven't used it for years."

Professor Higgins was a snob, however, his point that English is not spoken universally is important. Native speakers need to be wary of being patronizing by assuming a non-native speaker has made a mistake when in reality they have used a different version of English. Pronunciation is the least of the issues, as in the way Americans say Vite-tah-men and the Brits say Vit-tah-men. Differences also extend to vocabulary, spelling, and prepositions. While American English tends to be used in USA and South America, British English is used in commonwealth countries, Europe and world organizations. Multi-national firms based out of non-English speaking countries use a version of English as their language.

When a Japanese businessman took an assignment in Hungary, his English was criticized for not being European enough. His colleagues were not used to his vocabulary or syntax.

Vocabulary	Spelling	Prepositions
• Same word→ different definition: a rubber – a condom (US) or an eraser (UK) • Country specific words or phrases: 'committee was' (US) or 'committee were' (UK)	• Spell it with a 'z' or 's' → analyze/analyse; • Spelled with an 'o' or an 'ou' → color/colour; • Is there one 'l' or two → traveling/travelling • Sometimes just different → program (US) or programme (UK)	Prepositions can dramatically change the meaning of a sentence. For example more than sixteen combinations with 'look' create unique phrases e.g. look up to, look over, and look for. to the hospital (US) to hospital (UK)
Lists upon lists of examples exist, actually books of 'local language' have been written highlighting English variations.	It would be easy to assume that the author has made a mistake, but perhaps nothing could be further from the truth.	Those little words create nothing but problems in nearly all foreign languages.

> **TIP**
> **Use the words, spelling and phrases from the country of residence or company working language.**

Language variations are not exclusive to English; most of the major languages have dialects and/or country and regional differences. The Spanish spoken in South America, the Caribbean and parts of Europe is far from identical. The French spoken in Quebec is not the same as the French spoken in France; similarly, the Portuguese in Brazil has evolved differently from the Portuguese in Portugal.

> **WATCH OUT!**
> **Communicating in a second or third language is not an easy task; give people the benefit of the doubt.**

QUIZ – ENGLISH IS ENGLISH

1. Which of these is **not** one of the six official languages of the United Nations?
   a. Arabic
   b. English
   c. French
   d. Chinese
   e. German
   f. Spanish
   g. Russian

2. Which language is most widely spoken in the world?
   a. French
   b. English
   c. Chinese
   d. Spanish

3. How many official languages does South Africa have?
   a. One
   b. Four
   c. Seven
   d. Eleven

4. Match the words that have been adopted into the English language with the words' country or area of origin:

Word	Country or area of origin
Arsenal	Arabic
Giraffe	Hindi
Icon	Italy
Pajamas	Pacific Islands
Tattoo	Russian

5. Match the number of letters in the alphabet with the language:

Number of letters in alphabet	Language
Forty-six letters	Hawaiian
Twenty-four letters	Russian
Thirty-three letter	Greek
Eighteen letters	Finnish
Twenty-nine letters	Slovak

6. Which of these countries/territories does not list English as a national language?

   a. Malta
   b. Thailand
   c. Guam
   d. Canada
   e. South Africa

7. Sayings – sometimes colloquial sayings change during translation.

   a. When we are joking we might say someone's leg was pulled – what is tugged in Belgium?

   Arm   Foot   Finger

   b. When someone is very happy, they are said to be on cloud nine – what cloud are they on in Germany?

   Five   Seven   Eleven

What's the Weather Like Back Home?

The art of small talk is being able to have a conversation with a new acquaintance on a benign topic of which all parties have a basic knowledge. Richard Lewis, author of *When Cultures Collide*, notes that some cultures excel at small talk, the French and British for example, while others, such as Russians and Germans consider this 'frivolous' chatter and a waste of time. Conferences, cocktail parties, and business meals are places where casual conversation can be helpful. In which category do the subject matters fall?

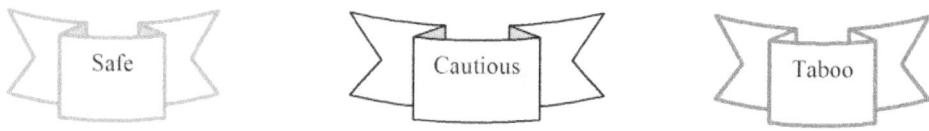

Safe

Some of the more accepted subject matters include:

- Weather
- Commuting and travel
- Entertainment, the arts and cultural activities such as the theater
- Hobbies
- Food and dining

As an example, nearly every country and even regions within a country have traditional dishes. People are usually proud of their local cuisine so consequently food is a good subject as long as it is discussed in a positive light. Visitors might criticize something they believe to be trivial within earshot of the wrong person and cause considerable offense. Dining out is a case in point. Consider the ramifications of this conversation between colleagues, one from the host country and the other visiting:

Colleague: I hope you are enjoying the meal.

Guest: Yes, the food is good.

Colleague: The next course will be served in about twenty minutes.

Guest: The next course? Service is a bit slow around here. How many courses are we having?

Colleague: Four or five. Delicious, isn't it? We should be finished around midnight.

Guest: Gosh, that's a bit late. We usually get through a meal in an hour back home. I guess that's okay. I had just hoped to answer emails tonight.

Colleague: Oh.

> **TIP**
> **Never insult or make disparaging comments about the topic being discussed.**

Cautious

Some people love to talk about their family, they carry pictures of their children or grandchildren so inquiring about family might be welcomed, but as Jan learned not everyone finds the topic acceptable:

> Jan of the Netherlands told the story of being introduced to George from Edinburgh, Scotland. Jan and George briefly talked about the weather and then Jan asked George about his family. George answered Jan's questions with single word responses. Jan was baffled by the situation as George had seemed friendly only a few minutes before. Jan decided to move the discussion in another direction and asked George about Scotland and golf. The conversation never died again. What Jan ascertained was that family was too personal for George to discuss with someone he had only met once.

There are those who would argue that work is a perfectly acceptable topic, but a number of cultures believe business or any subject related to work should not be broached until relationships have been established. Similar to work, some authors believe current events can be interesting to discuss, this is true as long as the matter is not contentious. Some topics such as health, family and vacation activities are viewed by some cultures as too personal for a casual conversation, sports can be inappropriate if an individual is particularly passionate about a sporting activity or team.

> **TIP**
> Ask open-ended questions, rather than those anticipating a yes or no answer as it encourages broader responses.

Taboo

Even if you like a lively debate, certain topics should be avoided unless you know the people well. Controversial matters do not belong in small talk conversations, especially as the banter can quickly turn heated and uncomfortable. Off-limit themes include:

- Religion
- Politics
- Money, chiefly personal finances
- Relationships and sex
- People's appearance or age

> **TIP**
> When all else fails, excuse yourself and walk away (this is better than offending someone with your comments).

QUIZ – WHAT'S THE WEATHER LIKE BACK HOME?

1. Put the following themes into the three small talk categories:

   Personal problems   Pets   Films   Technology   Mothers in-law
   Taxes   Economy   Trivia   Accomplishments   The boss
   Community event   Recent news article

Safe	Caution	Taboo

2. Small talk can be an effective way of networking and/or beginning a new relationship

   a. True
   b. False

3. The term 'politically correct', meaning taking special care not to offend anyone with what is said, originates from which country?

   a. Australia
   b. Canada
   c. Great Britain
   d. New Zealand
   e. United States of America

4. South Americans who attend business functions in which small talk is expected struggle to hold a conversation because of a language barrier

   a. True
   b. False

5. In which setting would small talk be unlikely?

   a. Cocktail party
   b. The middle of a meeting
   c. On an airplane
   d. During a meal with business associates
   e. During negotiations

6. Where is it illegal to deny the events of the Holocaust?

   a. USA
   b. Saudi Arabia
   c. Most European countries
   d. India
   e. China

7. In which country is it forbidden to criticize the King?

   a. Thailand
   b. The Netherlands
   c. Spain
   d. Sweden
   e. Libya

Getting the Message Right

Some people have a wonderful way with words but most of us just wish we did. There are those who depend on greeting cards to convey their sentiment but usually, and certainly in business, we have to find the right words ourselves. It is likely that at some time or another, the message you thought you communicated was misconstrued. Misunderstandings may be the result of the sender or the receiver. Some of the sources of problems:

- Language – one or both parties may not have a command of the language
- Vocabulary – word choice is too complex or not accurate, multiple meanings of the same word
- Expectations – preconceived notions (belief that sender and recipient think alike)
- Cultural variations – different meanings of the same information

Effective communication occurs when all parties make an effort to ensure the message was received as the sender intended.

Dalisay: Thank you for inviting me to your home.

Anika: My pleasure. I'm glad you could come.

Dalisay: You have a lovely home.

Anika: Thank you. Please come in and sit down. Would you like some coffee?

Dalisay: No thank you.

The ladies have a conversation about the neighborhood, their children and upcoming events. Dalisay wonders why Anika does not offer her coffee again. It does not occur to Anika to repeat the offer because Dalisay has already declined coffee. In the Philippines it is rude to accept an offer the first time, but on the third, Dalisay would have gladly accepted a cup of coffee. Anika, who is Dutch, assumed Dalisay would speak her mind.

Communication is paramount in our lives, whether expressing emotions, making a request or providing information. The message is sent through words, body language, intonation and silence; any of these can change the meaning. Add to the mix cultural variations, which can influence the interpretation of message, and miscommunications can and do happen. Everyone has the same goals; deliver a message, be polite and have the meaning and intent understood, however, both groups may be misinterpreted resulting in disappointment and frustration all around.

Edward T. Hall, author of *Beyond Culture, Cultural Differences and The Dance of Life,* among other titles, an anthropologist whose work focused on intercultural relations as well as non-verbal communication, first used the expressions 'high context' and 'low context' as labels to denote cultural communication differences. 'Low context' expressions are clear, direct and impersonal while 'high context' communication is indirect and the message is implied.

Low Context (LC)	High Context (HC)
Explicit/clear	Indirect/vague
Knowledge is more public	Relationship a priority
Goal oriented	Face-saving
Rational solutions, not personal ones	Common interest
Sense of urgency	Decision made face-to-face not in email

For example:

Jerry writes: Please provide the information by Friday, close of business.

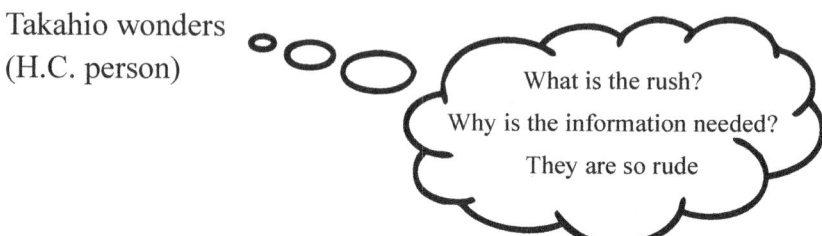

Takahio wonders (H.C. person)

What is the rush?
Why is the information needed?
They are so rude

Takahiro writes: The presentation is coming along nicely. We have appreciated the material provided by the group.

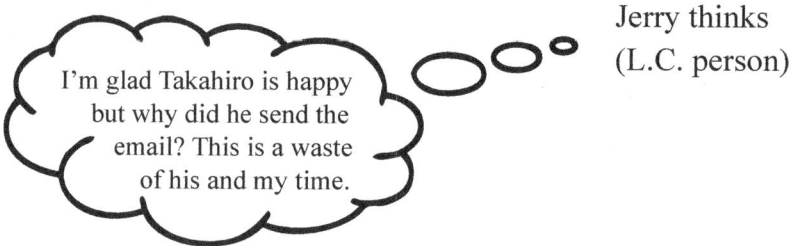

I'm glad Takahiro is happy but why did he send the email? This is a waste of his and my time.

Jerry thinks (L.C. person)

The concept of 'low' and 'high' context message is applicable to all forms of communication, including:

- Presentations
- Written communication, principally emails
- Meetings and negotiations
- One-on-one interactions

> **TIP**
> **Ensuring the meaning of a message is clear and received as intended is the responsibility of the originator of the message.**

QUIZ – GETTING THE MESSAGE RIGHT

1. Edward T. Hall developed his theories about communication while studying a tribe of Native Americans in the 1920s. Which tribe?

    a. Navajo
    b. Apache
    c. Sioux
    d. Cheyenne
    e. Inuit

2. Place the following countries in the category which best describes their communication style.

    Brazil   France   Germany   Hungary   Israel   Russia
    The Netherlands   USA

Low Context	High Context

3. Feedback – which of the following countries is comfortable giving negative feedback?

    a. Mexico
    b. India
    c. Australia
    d. Egypt
    e. Spain

4. The majority of cultures in the world are 'high context'

    a. True
    b. False
    c. It is about 50/50

5. Which words or phrases would more likely be written in an email?

    Would you mind   ASAP   Urgent   Perhaps   Deadline
        Appreciated   Please call me now

Low Context	High Context

6. Which is not a form of communication?

    a. Braille
    b. Sign language
    c. Morse code
    d. Reception
    e. Sounds

7. There is one phonetic alphabet

    a. True
    b. False

Thumbs Up

Facial expressions, body language and gestures can have a significant influence on the overall message being communicated. According to A. Barbour, author of *Louder Than Words: Nonverbal Communication*, actions may comprise of as much as 55% of your message. People in some cultures are very animated, while the body language of others is more subtle. As the intent and meaning of gestures and motions are not universal, it is advisable to know the basics of body language in order to send the right message and to enable you to interpret those directed at you.

Conveying someone has done a good job might be accomplished through a positive word, a nod of the head, a high-five, the okay sign, or thumbs up. If the recipient understands your intent, terrific, but it could be embarrassing if your message is interpreted as an insult, or worse, something vulgar.

Facial

The term 'poker face' is used to describe someone who does not show their thoughts or feelings on their face. This can be a deliberate tactic in competition or negotiations, but sometimes this is a cultural norm. You may think a smile has a lot of power, and is never misconstrued. Sadly, even a smile is not without its challenges.

> Robert was helping Leslie explain a problem to the receptionist. Robert wanted to reassure Leslie that everything would be fine so he smiled and winked at her. Immediately, Leslie turned red obviously quite uncomfortable and then she left the hotel lobby. Robert learned later that Leslie had interpreted the gestures as an invitation to join him in his room.

TIP
Watch other locals and see what facial expressions they use and what they mean. You may be surprised.

Body language

When communicating in another language, signs and signals can be essential to a successful exchange assuming the gestures have the same meaning to both parties. A nod of the head may mean 'no' not 'yes' and putting a finger to the temple might indicate a person is either thinking or that he thinks someone else is crazy. Personal space between people can be small or more than a meter. It depends on the relationship but also on culture; Latin and Middle Eastern cultures prefer to stand quite close to whomever they are talking to. Some gestures and behaviors may be completely ingrained in a person's conduct; the individuals may not realize they do it because it is so automatic.

> Joseph had been sitting in the tour bus for several hours and his legs were cramped. When the group entered the Buddhist temple and sat down as is customary, Joseph stretched out his legs with his feet facing the Buddha. A monk quickly motioned to him to change the position of his feet, moving them behind or under him. Joseph did not realize pointing the bottom of your feet at a Buddha was offensive in Thailand.

Sales personnel are taught to read body language as a part of their sales training, but these lessons can be irrelevant when selling cross-culturally. Comprehending the subtleties of the message is essential to an exchange.

Dual meanings

While gestures and signals can be effective communication tools, the second meaning of the gesture is frequently rude or obscene and therefore hazardous. Making a gesture that means the F-word is usually done in anger, for example in traffic when a driver has made a maneuver which irritates you. Here the gesture is made intentionally, problems arise when you want to say, for example, "Hello" or "Good job" but you use a gesture that is interpreted as vulgar.

A high school classmate had taught Romanian Gretel a gesture he told her meant 'hello'. He suggested she use it in Italy. The gesture was to take one hand and chop it into the fold of your arm (opposite your elbow) and close that arm upward making a fist. She made this gesture twice before one of members of the tour explained to her this was the equivalent of a thumbs-up (hitch hiker's thumb) in Romania or the middle finger in some countries.

TIP
Use gestures sparingly; know the meaning of the ones you use.

QUIZ – THUMBS-UP

1. There are several common methods of greeting used around the world, which of these is generally not used in business?

    a. Kiss
    b. Bow
    c. Handshake
    d. Hug

2. Which one of the following is not a gesture for beckoning someone (calling a person over) to you?

    a. One crooked finger (palm upward)
    b. One crooked finger (palm downward)
    c. Two or more fingers crooked (palm upward)
    d. Two or more fingers crooked (palm downward)

3. Where are the following gestures offensive:

Gesture	Country (s)
Thumbs up	United Kingdom
Okay	Iraq, Afghanistan
'V' sign	Thailand
Blow nose loudly	Mediterranean, Greece
Showing bottom of their feet	Japan

4. Showing appreciation is done in various ways – match the approach and the country:

Approach	Country (s)
Knock on table	Western Europe
Kissing fingers	Germany
Thumbs up	United States
Public recognition	Latin based countries

5. Match the preferred amount of space between people having a conversation:

Argentina   Bulgaria   Canada   Finland   Netherlands
Russia   Spain   Turkey   Uzbekistan   United Kingdom

Within an elbow's length/ touching	An arm's length/ no touching

Oh, Those Colorful Words We Learn

Young children learn to talk by mimicking others, particularly adults. It is embarrassing when children repeat obscenities their parents did not know the children had overheard. Toddlers are a bit like parrots, repeating words without knowing their meaning or impact; these little ones are just expanding their vocabulary.

It is not unusual for someone to admit they can only remember the swear words from a certain language. Perhaps because the obscene words are easy to say and recall. Or maybe because swear words are considered to be fun, especially when people around you may not understand. The challenge is that, as in the case of children, non-native speakers have no real feeling of the power of using the words or how offensive they may be to a native speaker.

> Watching crime/police dramas on German television (dubbed, of course) I learned several words and phrases very quickly:
>
> *Scheisse* = shit
>
> *Halten die Klapper* = shut-up
>
> Both these terms rolled easily off the tongue. However, I was quickly admonished as neither of these phrases is used during everyday conversation in Germany. I had no idea I was being offensive.

Dictionaries and official language-learning organizations consider the use of obscenities in any language to be crude and unacceptable in general company. If we take the case of the United States you may have noticed how the entertainment industry, through television programs, films and music, has given the world the impression that the use of obscenities is commonplace and acceptable in the US. Reality television shows are a major culprit. While this may be true to an extent, the non-native speaker is often unaware of the degree to which each word will cause offense.

> Three young German women on the subway were having a conversation about what words were acceptable and which ones were not. One stated she felt, "Bitch, Chienne and Schlampe were fine as long as you were with friends." (derogatory words for women in English, French and German, respectively). Another commented that she thought they were all rude but especially the German word *Schlampe*. The third had seen a funny t-shirt which said 'Shopping Bitch', so she felt this was okay. They seemed to agree that *Schlampe* was the worst, perhaps because it was in German, their own language, therefore stronger.

Saying the word 'F*#k' or using a gesture with the same meaning (see the Thumbs Up section for a bit more information) are not traditionally actions used by well-mannered people, however non-native speakers in some countries use them in 'family' television programs, commercials and on talk shows. A few examples:

- Morning radio DJs say "F*#k" in conversation
- Television characters or personalities use a version of the 'F-word' during prime-time shows
- An energy company has a character flip-off the camera

Do these people truly know how offensive their language and gestures are?

Some swear words are specific to a region so they may not be understood, and can be misunderstood by all native speakers of the same language. How many Americans knew the meaning of the film title *Austin Powers: The Spy Who Shagged Me* before they saw the film?

When using colorful language from another land it is not always easy to know who might be insulted. Be careful about using words and gestures that may verge on the edge of acceptability. If colorful language is used by a foreigner, remember that like a child, the non-native speakers may not understand the power and impact of their words.

> **TIP**
> **Find out what expletives are not acceptable in your host country. If in doubt, don't.**

QUIZ – OH, THOSE COLORFUL WORDS WE LEARN

1. Which of the following words does not have a vulgar meaning in British English?

    a. Shag
    b. Bugger
    c. Rubber
    d. Bollocks
    e. Randy

2. What type of humor is 'blue humor'?

    a. Puns
    b. Adult situations
    c. Sarcastic
    d. Irony
    e. Slapstick

3. Match the less offensive word with its corresponding expletive:

Less offensive	Offensive words
Shoot	Bitch
Darn, dang	Ass
Fudge, freaken, flip	Shit
Witch	Fuck
Butt	Damn

4. What is the meaning of the lyrics '*Voulez-vous coucher avec moi ce soir?*' in the song, *Lady Marmalade*?

   a. Would you like to sleep with me tonight?
   b. Will you be my boyfriend?
   c. Let's have sex, now
   d. Could we be friends?

5. Match the 'emphasis' words with their counterpart:

Emphasis Words	**Counterpart**
Horrible	Boring
Spectacular	Clean
Mundane	Good
Immaculate	Fine
Fabulous	Bad

Did You Hear The One About...?

Few would dispute the power of laughter, however, what each individual person finds funny varies significantly. Numerous factors including age, education, maturity level, even cultural background influences what tickles our fancy. For example, US Americans and British may both speak English but their senses of humor are quite different.

One audience might be amused while another remains confused and quiet depending on the subject of the joke. Political humor fails unless everyone knows the players and situation. A play on words only works if the audience understands the intricacies of the language, and trying to get a laugh using regional accents is rarely appreciated outside your home country.

> The voice of Mater in the animated film *Cars* has a very distinct accent with which a visual image of a likeable, down-home boy who is a bit naïve and gullible. Finding suitable accents in other languages to communicate the same qualities is not an easy task.

Humor can be particularly troublesome for presenters who have been taught to begin a presentation with a joke to put the audience at ease. The joke or comment might be misunderstood or misinterpreted causing the quip not only to be ineffective, but make the presenter look foolish.

> An American company Vice President was asked to make some opening remarks at an annual international customer forum. This southern gentleman began his presentation by saying, "I'm sure from my accent you know where I'm from". There was silence because few understood or appreciated the comment, most people in the room were not Americans.

As John Mole highlights in his book, *Mind Your Manners,* in some cultures, humor in the workplace is viewed as frivolous and diminishes the value of the message.

Numerous types of humor and comedy exist:

> Satire   Irony
> Play on words   Parody
> Self-effacing   Oxymoron   Gags
> Parody   Pranks   Slapstick   Puns   Physical
> antics   Funny stories   Riddles
> Off-color jokes   Practical jokes   Zany
> Exaggeration   Dry sense of humor   Witty
> Deadpan   Cartoons   Sarcasm

As author E.B. White once said, "Humor can be dissected as a frog can, but the thing dies…" If the joke must be explained, it does not work.

TIP
Do not try to translate jokes. They rarely survive.

QUIZ – DID YOU HEAR THE ONE ABOUT?

1. Carnival is a festive period in some parts of Germany; it is called *Fasching* and it ends on Fat Tuesday. A particular type of humor is common at the celebrations

    a. Political satire
    b. Self-effacing
    c. Pranks
    d. Irony

2. Which form of humor might be acceptable in a business setting?

    a. Satire
    b. Cartoon
    c. Gag (such as a whoopee cushion)
    d. Blue humor

3. Match the following form of humor with its use:

Humor	Commonly used
Satire	Film
Slapstick	Newspaper or magazine
Joke	Political humor
Cartoon	Television or film
Physical antics	Stand-up comedy

4. Match the definition and the word:

Definition	Word
Enjoy an activity	Funny
Something or someone that makes a person laugh	Fun
Hearty laugh	Funny bone
Spoof of a subject	Guffaw
Something that can be tickled by humor	Parody

5. Why should humor be avoided in business dealings?

   a. It may not put your audience at ease
   b. It may be misunderstood
   c. It may diminish the seriousness of your message
   d. All of the above

BUSINESS PRACTICES AND COMMUNICATION

May I Have Your Card, Please?

Meeting and greeting is an essential part of the initial phase of introductions. As previously mentioned, using the appropriate gestures and erring on the side of formality is advantageous, especially at preliminary meetings. Making a good first impression is important, and correct business card etiquette is an integral part of the early stage of relationship development. When working in, or with individuals from other countries, having business cards that conform to local standards is a good idea. Here are some basic features of business card etiquette which should be taken into consideration:

- Timing
- Handling
- Content
- Format/Style

Timing

Frequently, business cards are exchanged at the start of a meeting. This allows the participants to know the names and titles of the people with whom they are meeting and they can serve as an aid to remembering the participants' names. However, in the Scandinavian countries, Norway, Sweden, Denmark and Finland, handing them out at the end of the first meeting is commonplace.

Handling

In most cultures a business card should be treated with respect, but in Asia, card presentation is an art. Cards should be given with two hands, examined closely by the recipient and then set on the table. Business cards should not be put away, especially into a pocket and should never be written on.

Content

Contact details listed on a business card do not vary significantly in content between cultures. You will always put your name, title, company name and logo, address, phone numbers, email address and company website. In hierarchically-structured countries an important title such as 'Doctor' is crucial. In some countries, a person's education is another indication of competency, so listing university degrees is beneficial. Getting business cards printed in a local language is advisable when longer-term relationships are being developed, a common solution may be to print one side in English and the other in the local language.

Format/style

As well as cards printed in the local language, cards should also be the standard size for the country. Non-standard cards tend to be discarded more quickly because they are awkward to store.

> **WATCH OUT!**
> **Though technology is already beginning to change the way in which people exchange contact information, such as touching phone to phone (an application available from some manufacturers), until this practice is universal you will still need to have your business cards.**

QUIZ – MAY I HAVE YOUR CARD, PLEASE?

1. Business cards in a second language…?
    a. should be printed on another separate card
    b. should be printed on the reverse side of a card
    c. are really not necessary
    d. all of the above

2. In what color should Chinese business cards be printed?
    a. Red
    b. Yellow
    c. Gold
    d. Black
    e. Any color is fine

3. In the Middle East, business cards should be presented with…?
    a. the right hand
    b. the left hand
    c. both hands
    d. either hand, it does not matter

4. In the United States, the quality of the card stock used and embossed (raised lettering) is important?
    a. True
    b. False

5. Including a photo on your business card is commonplace in Africa?

    a. True
    b. False

6. What are the three primary ways people greet each other around the world?

    a. Shake Hands, Bow, Hug
    b. Kiss, Bow, Shake Hands
    c. Hug, Kiss, Bow
    d. Shake Hands, Bow, Curtsy

May I Call You Steve?

"Hey you!" is not the most polite way to get someone's attention. Addressing an individual by an appropriate name is important. In some countries people have a first and last name, while others have a series of names. Most of us are given a name at birth or soon after and occasionally people get to choose their own. Your name is usually carried with you for a lifetime. Some names are traditional while others are unique. There are those who go by a single name or their initials, nevertheless their identity is known in an instant; JFK, Mandela or Oprah. Names can convey information on heritage, religion, gender, perhaps ethnicity and even an era. Here are three things to think about regarding the use and importance of names:

- Significance
- Getting it Right
- Formality

Significance

The name a baby receives is a huge decision for parents. A number of expectant parents research and buy books about names. Many future mothers and fathers choose a family name to honor a parent or grandparent, others select a name with religious or ethnic significance, or a name to show the relationship of the child (son of, nephew of). Naming a child has great cultural significance.

> Jeri learned she was pregnant days after the twin towers collapsed in New York City. In keeping with a Jewish tradition to name a child after a recently departed family member, Jeri and her husband made the decision to name their newborn daughter after her cousin Vita, which means 'life', who had perished in the 9/11

disaster. Their newborn daughter, received the Hebrew name Chaia, meaning 'life.'

Some names reflect the feelings of the parents towards the child, but occasionally it is not positive, such as Nakusa or Nakushi, which in Hindi mean 'unwanted'.

The Associated Press reported in October 2011 that a renaming ceremony was being held in India for 285 girls who had the opportunity to select new names. A Safara (a region in India) health officer felt the renaming event was important to help fight future discrimination and to build the girls' self-esteem.

Getting it right

Names are important to individuals so getting it right is crucial. Pronunciation is not always easy because the letters are not universally spoken. Those familiar with Spanish know the 'j' is pronounced as a 'h' or 'w', however in Dutch the 'j' is pronounced like a 'y', so how would you pronounce 'Jesus'? Some languages enunciate each vowel or consonant-vowel combination such as Japanese, while other languages group multiple letters together to make sounds, for instance Polish and Greek.

Determining someone's gender by their name can be a challenge and create problems when you first communicate with someone by email. Knowing which is the first name and which is the surname is not always evident. Addressing someone correctly is essential in business; assumptions can be risky, particularly regarding gender.

> **TIP**
> **Inquire about or research a new name, before addressing someone in person or in writing.**

Formality

Using titles such as Mr. and Mrs. when formally addressing elders, professionals and senior members of staff was common in the United

States until the late 1960s. Today some professors, and most physicians, have held onto their titles but they are the exception. US Americans have adopted what many consider to be a very informal communication style and use first names almost from the outset. While first names are commonplace in the US and in the UK, titles are standard in many other parts of the world. Be sure to check.

> Greet, a Belgian Vice President of Business Development, recounts the story of bringing a group of US businessmen to Switzerland in 2010 to discuss a potential business venture. These businessmen addressed their Swiss counterparts by their first names, asked personal questions and conducted business informally. The Swiss contingent decided rather quickly this was not a group with whom they wanted to do business.

Using first names before being invited to do so is viewed as presumptuous, getting the business association off to a bad start or ending opportunities.

TIP
Ask a person how they want to be addressed at the start of a business meeting. Only shorten a name or use a nickname after being asked to.

Nationalities

Nearly as important as a person's name, other ways we reference an individual are key. Some terms are obviously offensive and others more subtle. Asking a Scot or an Aussie if they are an Englishman, calling a Jewish person a Jew or referring to a country, especially a former colony, by an earlier name will not ingratiate you with others.

During my research I heard an interview with Dean Foster, a modern cultural expert who stated that some South Americans, particularly Brazilians, resent that the term American is exclusively reserved for citizens of the United States when in fact anyone from North, Central or South America should have the right to use the term. They consider themselves inhabitants of a country in the Americas too.

Most nationalities have one of three endings, 'an', 'ish' or 'ese', although exceptions exist. There are a few countries that have names which include the word 'United' or 'Republic' which makes identifying the nationality more challenging:

Country	Nationality
People's Republic of China	Chinese
Republic of Macedonia	Macedonian
United Arab Emirates	Emirati

Citizens of the United States are referred to as US citizens in some official resources, but they will most likely continue to be referred to as Americans.

> **TIP**
> **If in doubt add the letters 'US' to the term American, as I have done in this book.**

Titles are so important in Germany that a person may be addressed by more than one. The chancellor, Angela Merkel, should officially be addressed as Mrs. Dr. Merkel. In some countries a suffix is added to the name as a sign of respect. Asking staff and business associates to address you by Mr. Ms. or Dr. is your prerogative. However, as Gwyneth Olofsson, author of *When in Rome or Rio or Riyadh...* reminds us, it is important in egalitarian societies such as the New Zealand to treat people with the same level of respect you insist upon yourself.

> **WATCH OUT!**
> **If you want to be referred to as Mr. Sanchez, then call administrative personnel Mr. Kinkaid or Ms. Otis.**

QUIZ – MAY I CALL YOU STEVE?

1. Which world leader required people to register in their communities and to provide both a first and last name?
   a. Julius Caesar
   b. Alexander the Great
   c. Napoleon Bonaparte
   d. King Henry VIII

2. When introducing a man in Indonesia, what is included with the name as a show of respect?
   a. Meneer
   b. Singh
   c. San
   d. Pan
   e. Bupak

3. In which country do women use the surname of their husband after marriage?
   a. Korea
   b. Belgium
   c. Peru
   d. Cambodia
   e. Iceland

4. When writing a person's full name, the last name is always written last.
   a. True
   b. False

5. Some names are given to both men and women; which name is not transgender?
   a. Jan
   b. Jean
   c. Kelly
   d. Nicola
   e. Anika

6. From which Asian country is it not uncommon for the inhabitants to take an English first name?
   a. South Korea
   b. Japan
   c. China
   d. Laos
   e. Thailand

7. Dual citizenship is only allowed in one of the following countries?
   a. Monaco
   b. Andorra
   c. United States
   d. Angola
   e. China

8. Children born in a country are automatically citizens in that country.
   a. True
   b. False

9. Governmental concerns about dual nationality include all of the following except?
   a. Military Service
   b. Residency
   c. Taxation
   d. Treason
   e. Voting

Round the Clock

How people and cultures view time is significantly different; consider the child who thinks the school day will never end or the career woman who believes 'there are not enough hours in the day'. It is sometimes assumed perceptions of time vary mainly between Eastern and Western cultures, but delving further into the concept of time it becomes apparent this is an oversimplification. In fact, Richard Lewis, author of *When Cultures Collide,* describes three categories of time:

- Linear
- Multi-active
- Circular

Linear

In cultures such as Austria and Australia time is viewed as a timeline with a beginning and an end. Time and activities move forward in an organized manner; schedules and hard work lead to success. Meetings begin promptly, deadlines are adhered to, and industriousness and productivity are rewarded. Some countries have a linear thought process related to time, but it is a hybrid system where 'privileged' individuals, such as found in a monarchy, have advantages because of who they are and their connections over individuals who simply work hard.

Multi-active

In these cultures, such as Brazil, Turkey and Spain, schedules should not dictate time, if a conversation is not complete but the scheduled time is up, this is not a reason to stop talking. The philosophy is to focus on the activity or people at hand, giving them the respect they are due before moving onto the next subject. This means when meetings, deadlines or decisions are postponed this is part of the natural course of doing business so getting annoyed or upset make little sense.

Circular

In places such as China, Thailand and the Native American culture, the sun rises, the sun sets, babies are born, people die; life is a cycle of events. The past influences today and will impact the future, the past cannot be ignored. In business terms this means the deal on the table (current negotiations) has some value, but it is only one part of a much bigger picture. In these cultures business relationships are developed over time, sometimes from generation to generation, so a fabulous 'one time' offer would not be of interest.

> **TIP**
> Take something with you to occupy your time while you wait but develop patience and flexibility.

Attitudes toward time affect various aspects of getting things accomplished or doing business:

- Punctuality
- Setting and/or meeting deadlines/commitments
- Decision making

Gwyneth Olofsson relays the story of a Swedish director arriving late to a meeting that his subordinate manager was holding. He was unable to join because the door had been locked. The manager was not reprimanded but praised for his respect for time. Conversely, the King of Ghana in 2003, kept British reporters at a scheduled news conference waiting nearly five hours. The reporters were frustrated but the king seemed unconcerned. Vastly different mindsets.

> **TIP**
> Be punctual for appointments and meetings – even in countries renowned for being tardy the expectation is the guest waits, not the host.

QUIZ – ROUND THE CLOCK

1. Idioms – match the idiom with its definition:

Idiom	Definition
Take your sweet time	Something is reliable and not just a trend
Stand the test of time	A long time
Time of your life	A long quiet period usually after a surprising or embarrassing comment
A month of Sundays	Enjoy yourself
Pregnant pause	Do something at your own pace

2. Which of the following sets of neighboring countries do not have polar opposite views on time?

    a. USA and Mexico
    b. Switzerland and Italy
    c. Poland and Romania
    d. Japan and Thailand
    e. Finland and Russia

3. Decision Making – match the time with the decision making outcome:

Time	Decision Making Outcome
Linear	Made some headway but more work to be done in the following days
Multi-Active	Items discussed, no immediate decisions, some items eventually done others deemed unnecessary
Circular	Desired tasks accomplished

4. Put the following countries in the category which best reflects the culture's attitude toward time.
Austria   Bolivia   Hungary   India   Kuwait   New Zealand
Nigeria   Sweden   Vietnam   Thailand   USA

Linear	Multi-active	Circular

5. "Yesterday is gone; tomorrow has not yet come. We have only today. Let us begin". Who is credited with this quote?

   a. John F. Kennedy
   b. Mother Teresa
   c. Winston Churchill
   d. Oscar Wild
   e. Elizabeth Barrett Browning

6. Some cultures believe consulting their ancestors is essential before embarking on major decisions; which time philosophy?

   a. Linear
   b. Multi-active
   c. Circular
   d. All of the above

Substance vs Style

When asked which is more important, substance or style, most people would answer 'substance'. Perhaps this is the correct answer, but in reality the significance of appearance should not be underestimated. It creates a first impression and influences the memorability of the message. In cooking and in business the value of a quality presentation must not be dismissed.

Some chefs believe food presentation is an essential component of the gastronomic experience. On the other hand, some people believe taste is paramount and the presentation of the food is simply a bonus. US Americans love their turkey dressing/stuffing served at Thanksgiving, but to a stranger it may not be a particularly visually appetizing dish. French cuisine looks fabulous on a plate, but the portions are notoriously small. Each approach has its place and its fans.

Facts, Figures and Graphs

Business men and women from some cultures insist upon presentations which include tables of figures and complicated graphs, Germans and the Japanese are partial to this style. Substance and all relevant supporting data are placed on slides, frequently exceeding the number able to be presented in the designated timeslot.

> Debby, a trainer and marketing consultant from the Netherlands, was presenting to a group of relocation experts about the benefits of using social media for business development. One of her slides had several columns of data including a list of the countries in the world (192), their population and Internet penetration. She said to the audience of 60, "As you can see Hungary has a penetration of x%". No one in the room could read the figures on the slide.

Presenting within your own country or corporate culture may allow you to use this style, but it is not advisable in multicultural settings.

One regional director sought assistance for a communication issue on behalf of his team. The points, which included innovative ideas, strategies and challenges from the European work teams, were not making an impact on top management. The US management struggled to understand the message due to the style of presentation and, to a lesser degree, its language use.

Style

Style does not mean 'fluff' – a quality presentation has a purpose, a message, supporting facts, considers the audiences' position and is well practiced. The slides or other multimedia support should complement the presenter but not take over. Tony Luna, author of *Six Elements of an Effective Presentation*, lists the following components:

1. Point of view
2. Continuity
3. Professionalism
4. Simple message
5. Uniqueness
6. Relevance to the audience

In both scenarios the business associates have material and information they need to communicate, but how the message is conveyed influences how the message is received. Generally, cultural differences must be respected, but in the case of presentations to multicultural audiences, I highly recommend learning the techniques of an effective presentation, using them and not falling back into old habits.

> **TIP**
> **Focus on the audience and what is important to them, and less on what you want or need to tell them.**

QUIZ – SUBSTANCE VS STYLE

1. All of the following elements are essential to a presentation except?

    a. Clear message

    b. Value to audience

    c. Opening joke

    d. Facts

    e. All of the above should be included

2. When speaking to a Japanese audience, which of the following is important?

    a. Be formal

    b. Provide convincing facts, with lots of supporting data with corresponding graphics

    c. Do not pressure for a decision

    d. Allow time for questions

    e. All of the above

3. Which country prefers a presentation with 'bells and whistles'?

    a. Finland

    b. England

    c. USA

    d. Australia

4. When giving a presentation in which country might interruptions be common?

   a. Brazil
   b. South Africa
   c. Belgium
   d. Poland

5. If you are presenting in China and some of the material is challenged, this is done to undermine you

   a. True
   b. False

One Size Fits All

Being able to standardize processes and products has advantages, avoiding the necessity for starting each project from the ground up, encouraging the implementation of 'best practices' and helping ensure everyone is 'on the same page.' While standardization has its benefits, downsides exist. Some of the disadvantages include local customer expectations being overlooked, product types and size not being universal, and local business practices and laws differing from the 'norm'.

> A t-shirt that says 'one size fits all' is terrific for some women but when you are on the petite side, the shirt makes a better nightshirt. Perhaps because standard women's socks in the USA are size 9-11 (or 37-42 on the continent), the heels of the socks do not stay at the heels of women with smaller feet but sit at their ankles. The concept that 'one size fits all' is puzzling.

Haute couture, customized furniture or one-of-a-kind items are not particularly accessible to the average consumer because they are cost prohibitive. Buying 'off-the-rack' and knowing others have purchased similar products, is not an issue for the average consumer. Some businesses pride themselves on selling consistent products and services and have been very successful. Many chain restaurants and stores have developed a model which works for them and is reproduced in every location. The benefits of consistency, uniformity, and economies of scale are believed to outweigh any advantages of local variation. While this philosophy may work within a country, it is frequently challenged beyond its borders.

Advertising

Whether it is a product, an advertising campaign, or a style of doing business, mistakes in business can be costly, for example, the costs of a product recall or tarnishing a firm's reputation.

Coors Brewing Company ran an advertisement with the slogan, "Turn it Loose" which when translated into Spanish was "Suffer from diarrhea."

> **TIP**
> **Slogans and images rarely effectively translate directly, use professional translators – having a translation verified by a third party can help avoid small but significant mistakes.**

Successes

Most businesses that are able to penetrate markets outside their home countries are successful because they modify their products, services and marketing to fit local expectations or standards. Some fast food chains, hotels and product manufacturers have excelled in this area. Strategies adopted by these successful organizations include:

- Franchise
- Joint venture with a local company
- Utilization of local experts

While standardization is paramount to McDonald's, its success around the world comes from using the above strategies and because they offer local foods and advertises in the local language.

> **WATCH OUT!**
> **Do not assume what works in one country will work in another. Research how other companies like yours have fared, and talk to local experts who have a knowledge of your culture and product and those of the target location.**

Learn from mistakes

When a company expands into a new market, doing things the 'tried and true' way may not sit well with residents or target customers. When this happens consider who is likely to be prepared to adapt – your company or your potential customers?

The highly successful Disney organization struggled when it first entered the European market near Paris, France.

- Wine was not available at midday, a beverage regularly drunk at lunch by many Frenchmen
- The Disney hotel rates were higher than the market would bear
- Beards and facial hair were against the dress code of employees

EuroDisney's leadership team decided the European market was important and given they had already made a substantial investment, modifying a few business practices made good business sense.

> **TIP**
> **Do not expect potential customers to change to accommodate you.**

Failures

Taking risks and trying the untested/unproven is a philosophy some cultures embrace. While the rewards can be substantial, the failures can be equally costly. High-profile flops have not been limited to US firms, who ventured into new markets and then struggled to attain their goals.

- Walmart's advancement into Germany and South Korea were fraught with challenges:
    - In Germany local laws restricted the way they did business, including opening hours and loss-leaders, and their overly friendly staff were not regarded as genuine

- In South Korea some of the display shelves in the Walmart stores were too high, so customers had to use ladders to reach the products. Additionally, the multi-pack items such as shampoo and bigger bags of rice were unpopular because they were not easily transported without a car. Many of the shoppers came by foot or traveled on public transportation.

- Marks & Spencer leapt into the continent, but the loyalty they experienced in the UK did not follow them

- Charitable organizations not involving local leadership or considering the hierarchy within the regions see their projects succeed at first blush, but long-term results are much less impressive

---

WATCH OUT!
**The cultural aspects of overseas business should not be considered as soft, therefore unimportant.
Ignore them at your peril!**

QUIZ – ONE SIZE FITS ALL

1. What did McDonald's do to be successful in India?

    a. Taught the local residents the value of eating beef
    b. Created an extensive vegetarian menu
    c. Prepared its French fries in a special oil
    d. Opened it restaurants round the clock

2. Which of the following is **not** a location of Disney's theme parks?

    a. Orlando
    b. Anaheim
    c. Hong Kong
    d. Paris
    e. Sao Paulo

3. Which of the following mergers/acquisitions struggled with cultural clashes?

    a. Alcatel-Lucent
    b. Exxon-Mobil
    c. Price-Waterhouse
    d. Glaxo-SmithKline

4. According to Mike Gomez, managing partner at Allegro Consulting, what percentage of foreign businesses fail in the United States?

   a. 100%
   b. 90%
   c. 75%
   d. 60%
   e. 45%

5. Which product was **not** a dud for Walmart?

   a. Oblong pillowcases in Germany
   b. Golf clubs in Brazil
   c. Ice skates in Mexico
   d. Rice in South Korea
   e. Chinese products in Japan

Where to Draw the Line?

Everyone has a moral compass that guides them, based on their fundamental values. Each person has to decide what is tolerable and intolerable for him or herself, and where to draw their own line. Individuals must decide if conforming to the 'norm' is morally 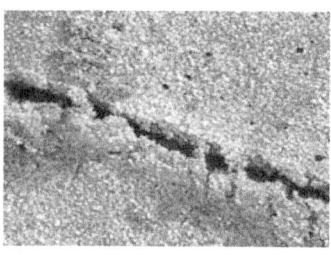 acceptable to them. Some must determine what they are willing to do to achieve a goal (pushing boundaries). Likewise, many companies have a code of ethics outlining appropriate and inappropriate behavior for the company and its staff. Employees are usually required to sign a document acknowledging and agreeing to these guidelines. Conflicts can arise when conducting business within your own country, but add cultural differences and the lines can get very blurred. Consider the following:

- When the choice is between obeying the law and supporting a friend, what does a person do?
- Is it the responsibility of the company to send out correct invoices or the responsibility of the customer to check them?
- What does a company wanting to expand into a new market do, when they receive information that their request to conduct business will be granted if they support a local project, such as installing an air conditioning system in a local museum?
- What should a person do if they receive a gift from a business associate they find offensive or inappropriate?
- As a matter of integrity, are you required to disclose everything to government officials?

The values of a culture influence the answer. People need to be able to live with a clear conscience.

> **TIP**
> **Follow your own personal compass because you will be held accountable.**

Even if a person wants to follow the law, there are times when you will find that laws are in direct conflict with each other. How can you know which one takes precedence? The following case study illustrates this:

> Ellen, an American married to an Italian, is struggling because she is caught between two legal systems. US Treasury officials require disclosure of all financial assets and say that if the cumulative amount of personal funds in foreign bank and financial institutions is over $10,000.00 which includes banking accounts Ellen has signature authority on for companies or organizations. Ellen and her Italian husband have several joint accounts in Italy, which the US government would expect her to report, however Italian law requires permission from all principal parties before data can be released. Her husband sees no value in giving consent. What must Ellen do? Many expatriates have similar dilemmas.

> **TIP**
> **Get professional advice from each country involved whenever you come across a potential conflict.
> Get informed before you make your decision.**

QUIZ – WHERE TO DRAW THE LINE

1. In which country would family **not** take priority when making a business decision?

    a. China
    b. Pakistan
    c. Turkey
    d. Canada
    e. Venezuela

2. Gift giving – match the gift and the country in which it should **not** be given:

Gift	Country
Knife	Switzerland
Clock	Belarus
Items with large company logos	France
Anything in groups of four	Brazil
Caviar	Japan

3. Which of these prominent people has **not** been convicted of wrong doing in their justice system?

    a. Jacques Chirac
    b. Silvio Berlusconi
    c. Saddam Hussein
    d. Julian Assange

4. Some cultures struggle with the 'bottom-line' orientation of other cultures.

   a. True
   b. False

5. Brooks Peterson, author of *Cultural Intelligence,* suggests putting ethical questions into a matrix to help evaluate situations – where would you place the following topics?

   - Changing a contract in the middle of a project
   - Women negotiating deals
   - Treatment of animals in research
   - Insider dealing

	Legal	Illegal
Ethical		
Unethical		

Are You Hiring?

Lifetime employment still exists in some places, but it is becoming less common as companies face challenging economic times. Mergers and acquisitions change the landscape and employees are tempted by other opportunities. When an individual is looking for employment in another country, either by choice or circumstance, some important factors must be taken into consideration:

- Preparation of a locally-styled résumé or Curriculum Vitae (CV)
- Face to face interview
- Fluency in the host language
- Ease of obtaining a work permit

Résumé or Curriculum Vitae (CV)

Both terms are used to describe that essential document reflecting who you are and what you have to offer an employer. All résumés include your work history, but other elements of a CV are not universal. While secondary education or university diplomas are adequate in most countries a few places are interested in primary/grade schools too. Job titles, education vernacular and other professional certifications do not always easily translate and may require explanation. Personal information, for example: name, contact details, hobbies and organization activities may be provided, but in some places more is required including age, marital status, number of children and nationality.

> In France, the university a young person attends makes a huge difference to the doors that will open and their career potential. Edwin, an Iranian engineer, was applying to graduate school in order to get a Master's in Business Administration (MBA), but his list of graduate schools was short; his philosophy being 'attend the best or attend none'. When he initially applied to INSEAD (a prestigious graduate program in France) he was not accepted.

> **TIP**
> Confirm the number of pages your CV should contain before you send it in and find out if they expect a photograph.

Interview

Being well prepared and making a positive first impression may go without saying, but these two components are critical. Arriving 15 to 30 minutes early to an appointment starts the candidate off on the right foot even in multi-active countries. An interview should be used to expand on your attributes. Being able  to articulate your strengths without appearing arrogant is essential. When you are interviewing for a multinational firm you may be asked to clarify aspects of your résumé which the interviewer may not be familiar with, such as Valedictorian, A-levels or trade school.

> One of the biggest challenges for applicants, who have been taught to be humble, is coming across as confident and expressing their strengths. They can easily tell you the positive attributes of others, but they are less comfortable answering the same question about themselves. They feel it is egotistical, while other cultures view it as confident and evidence of 'selling oneself' to their potential new employer.

> **WATCH OUT!**
> Never be critical of anything especially your previous employer, even if the interviewer seems empathetic.

Language

Even if the corporate language is English, being able to speak at least two languages is an asset to any job candidate. As Gwyneth Olofsson clearly explains in her book, *When in Rome or Rio or Riyadh...,* companies recognize the effort a person has gone to in order to learn a second language, and they believe it demonstrates an open mind and interest in another culture.

One of the complaints about former Alcatel-Lucent CEO, Patricia Russo of the USA, was that she never learned to speak any French.

> TIP
> **Fluency is not mandatory but a working knowledge of a language is appreciated as a skill.**

Permits

Most countries require a visa, residence permit or both as prerequisites to employment for foreigners. As the name implies, the bureaucracy associated with working in a country other than your home country is usually complex. In addition, these regulations may have rules that apply to one group, such as inhabitants from other European locations, or family members of residents, but which are not applicable to others. Employers may try to help but because individuals have their own set of conditions it is not always 'black and white.'

> WATCH OUT!
> **Learn the regulations yourself and consider legal assistance.**

QUIZ – ARE YOU HIRING?

1. A study conducted by Outplacement consultants in Chicago (2005) found that the number of months it took for someone to find a new job was equal to_____?

    a. Age divided by 10
    b. Age divided by 5
    c. Salary divided by 20,000
    d. City population divided by 250,000

2. What is the difference between a résumé and curriculum vitae (CV) in the United States?

    a. There is no difference, the terms are interchangeable
    b. A résumé is the term used for hourly paid employees and a CV is used by salaried employees.
    c. A résumé is used in the business community and a CV is used in the academic world.
    d. The term résumé is used by all employers, the term CV is rarely uttered.

3. Some countries are conducting research on how putting your name on a CV can influence candidate selection? Why?

    a. There is concern candidates are being discriminated against because of their ethnic name.
    b. It is believed candidates are receiving preferential treatment because of their name.
    c. There is a concern that family members of students are receiving preferential treatment.
    d. It is believed candidates with shorter names are preferred to names with more than ten letters.

4. What do Wharton, INSEAD and Fundação Dom Cabral have in common?
   a. They are all located in the Americas
   b. They produce highly sought after MBA graduates
   c. They are all Ivy League schools
   d. They are colleges at Oxford

5. What challenges might applicants face when seeking employment in a foreign country?
   a. Work permit
   b. Ethnic discrimination
   c. No reciprocity for credentials
   d. Language skills
   e. All of the above

Accompanying Partner or Trailing Spouse

Dual careers and two-income households have increased in the last 35 years, primarily in industrialized nations where more opportunities exist for women in the workplace. Plus many families believe that money is needed in order to maintain their lifestyle choice. Couples are used to juggling household responsibilities and career demands and the system works fine until one of the pair is offered an international assignment. Once the equation changes, one has new a job and responsibilities and is busy all week, while his/her spouse is in a completely new position without a support network, uncomfortable with an unfamiliar identity and perhaps a lack of purpose. Will this be a great adventure or huge disaster? The spouse/partner will have a multitude of challenges, such as:

- Identity crisis
- Financial dependence
- Fending for him/herself
- Isolation

Identity crisis

A person's identity is grounded in his/her culture, but work and family play a significant role. Individuals who have built a successful, rewarding career cannot easily abandon it. Making the decision to take a sabbatical or give up a career is heart wrenching, but living with the choice is even more difficult.

> Greek was Varvara's first language, her second German, her third English and she was studying Russian in St. Petersburg, Russia, when she met Alexander an Irish/American also studying abroad. Varvara earned a doctorate in education and Alexander joined the Foreign Service. Varvara said, she, "did not want to waste" all of her years of study so the first few years of their marriage she chose to stay in Germany rather than moving with Alexander to Azerbaijan or Oman.

> **TIP**
> **It takes time to adjust to a new location, usually about six months. Culture shock is part of your transition, so be prepared for it and know what you are going through is normal.**

As Andrea Martins, founder of the support website *www.expatwomen.com* and the publisher of *Expatriate Women: Confessions* anthology, suggested in a presentation at the 2010 FAWCO conference, women can use their career break to further their education, start a new business, research a business opportunity or do whatever they want to help them be their own person.

> Belen, her husband and three daughters moved from Ecuador to Europe so that he could expand his employer's presence. Belen took advantage of not working to develop her hobby, photography. They have returned to Ecuador and she is still an avid photographer.

Financial dependence

Another factor contributing to an identity crisis is financial dependence. Although the expatriate package may be generous and the loss of a second income may have a minimal effect on the family's financial situation, being financially dependent on another person for the first time in years can be distressing for the spouse affected. For many this is a hard pill to swallow and it can be made worse when the term 'allowance' mentioned.

> **TIP**
> **Have frank conversations about roles, responsibilities and expectations ahead of time.**

Fending for him/herself

Whether managing the household affairs was your primary responsibility before the relocation or this is a new position, doing so in another country, usually in another language is not as easy as you might expect. The way in which these tasks are accomplished may be different, time required is frequently longer and the chances of being misunderstood are great. Consequently, what your partner might view as simple is often frustrating and stressful.

> If the person behind the deli counter asks a patron to repeat their order when the customer is in their own country, the customer assumes the clerk was distracted or just didn't hear. When the same scenario occurs when a person is communicating in a foreign language, they assume they made a mistake. This does not help someone's self-esteem or stress level.

Isolation

When people are faced with challenging situations, having encouragement from family and friends can be a huge help. Unfortunately, relocation to a new place, even in your home country means functioning without your established support system. Some people will develop new friendships and utilize modern modes of communication to lessen the feelings of isolation and separation, but be mindful of the more negative consequences that can occur, depression and/or substance abuse.

TIP
Get out there and get involved:
- **Find and join a club of people who are living in a similar situation**
- **Identify schools and organizations that offer creative outlets**
- **Get involved in the community**
- **Join a language group (new or existing language)**

In the end accompanying partners must decide whether they are going to become what is often called 'a trailing spouse', or the new term, coined by Apple Gidley at the 2011 Families in Global Transition – STARS (Spouse Travelling and Relocating Successfully). The employed partner's choice to take an international assignment can have an enormous impact on your family's happiness, but don't forget you still have a choice.

QUIZ – ACCOMPANYING PARTNER OR TRAILING SPOUSE?

1. Which of the following words/phrases is **not** used to describe a committed relationship between two adults?

    a. Spouse

    b. Partner

    c. Significant other

    d. Companion

    e. Mate

2. Match the year in which divorce became legal in the corresponding country:

Country	Year
Philippines	Still illegal
Argentina	1987
Ireland	1997
Jordan	1939
United Kingdom	1530

3. Common myths about an international assignment include?

    a. Family is a priority for the employee's company

    b. Getting a work permit in another country will be easy

    c. The adjustment period in a new location is less than one month

    d. Life will be the same or better just in another location

    e. All of the above

4. Match the idiom to the meaning:

Idiom	Meaning
A ball and chain	Feel obligated to marry due to pregnancy
My better half	The person is a burden
Shotgun wedding	No obligations
Marriage (match) made in heaven	The person is an asset, usually a spouse or significant other
Footloose and fancy free	The situation is very positive

5. Fifty percent of the accompanying spouse/partners are male?

   a. True
   b. False

EVERYDAY LIVING

Do the Numbers Add Up?

1 Is it a one or a seven? Is it a nine or the letter 'g'? At an early age children learn to write their numbers and letters. While variations in alphabets are expected, more consistency is anticipated when dealing with numbers. Differences exist, whether it is how the numbers are written, the format of the information or what the figures are meant to communicate. Not all dates are written: month, date, year; the Gregorian calendar is not used in all cultures, telephone numbers and addresses do not have a standard format and the placement of a comma or period can change value.

Dates

Similar to names, dates can be very important both personally and professionally. Anniversaries and public holidays, and the deadline date for filing taxes in your respective countries have a role in people's lives. Dates are essential to anyone for scheduling appointments, arranging meetings and holding conference calls. Sometimes dates are written in words but more often, they are written in numeric form. This is not a problem as long as everyone knows in which order the elements are being presented. What date is, 12/09/11? Is it December ninth 2011, the twelfth of September 2011 or the eleventh of September 2012?

- European Date = Day Month Year
- American Date = Month Day Year
- Japanese Date = Year Month Day

> **TIP**
> **When making appointments by email or letter always spell out the month and write the year in full. Include the time zone on appointment times.**

Addresses and telephone numbers

People are regularly asked to provide their address, phone number, email address or other pertinent information when making a reservation, ordering an item, or leaving a message. It is essential this data is accurate and legible. Challenges arise when someone writes the figures in a different style or format to the one the recipient is used to. There are four numbers written in various forms that are not always easily identifiable to someone from another culture: one, seven, four and nine.

In this digital age this poses a challenge for phone number and address formats, which are far from universal. This is especially frustrating when attempting to provide required information in pre-formatted forms, particularly on websites. It is aggravating when companies, universities, and other organizations claim to provide services to international patrons, but their systems have not been upgraded to handle the formats of those international customers.

> Tal, an Israeli high school senior in Belgium, was applying to universities in the United States through the university on-line application process. She had trouble with nearly every application because her address and four-digit zip code were non-standard as far as the system was concerned.

TIP
Companies and institutions need to provide systems that support internationally formatted data if they have international clients.

Punctuation

The small . has several names and corresponding meanings:

- Dot = Internet addresses and email addresses
- Point = numerically
- Period or full stop = sentence punctuation

In the US and the UK the point is written between dollars and cents or between pounds and pence but in continental Europe this same mark is used to designate thousands and the comma is used between the euros and cents. A misplaced comma or point could make a huge difference in the price of something.

$12.00 = twelve dollars

$1,200.00 = twelve hundred dollars

€12,00 = twelve euro

€12.000,00 = twelve thousand euro

While numbers and the punctuation used in equations are small the mistakes and misunderstanding can be enormous, so it is important to know which ones the group is working with. Since so much is riding on the digits, it is imperative to ensure they are accurately written, read and interpreted.

> **TIP**
> **Always double check your online entries before confirming them and pressing SEND.**

QUIZ - DO THE NUMBERS ADD UP?

1. Write today's date numerically for each country?

   The United States _____

   Europe   _____

   Japan   _____

2. Match the international country calling code and their corresponding country:

Calling codes	Country
30	Greece
254	Kenya
51	Peru
60	Malaysia
354	Iceland

3. When dialing a country other than the US, a person must dial 00 plus the country code or one can select a symbol instead of pressing 00. What is the symbol?
   a. =
   b. –
   c. *
   d. +
   e. #

4. Match zip codes (postal codes) to the country:

Zip/Postal codes	Country
200040	Netherlands
1016 GZ	United Kingdom
2609	Qatar
SW1X 7RN	China
None used	Australia

5. Match the number 'idioms' with their meaning:

Idiom	Meaning
Count your lucky stars	Very happy
Take five	Recognize the positive aspects of your life
Someone's days are numbered	Raise your expectations too soon and disappointment may occur
Don't count your chickens before they hatch	Take a break
The person is on cloud nine	Very little time is left in a situation (e.g. might be laid off)

The Devil's in the Details

Being detailed-oriented is an essential quality of some professions. People want their neurosurgeons, engineers, architects and pilots to be meticulous in their work. Most individuals prefer to leave the particulars to those who are more methodical. However, if you have ever mistyped an email address, paid exorbitant fees for texting from another country or not been able to plug in your charger for phone, razor and so on, then you know how important the details are, even to the average person in day to day life.

Electronics

Many business travelers and vacationers are aware that small appliances do not have universal plugs and they may be 110v or 220v. Travelers often carry a convertor or transformer so their curling irons or computer chargers can be plugged into any outlet. Frustration occurs when something appearing identical is not.

> Alan, visiting for Oktoberfest from Iowa, travels light so he did not have his PC with him so he used the computer of his friend to check his email. Responding to his emails was not as easy as he had expected because some of the letters were not located in the same spots on the keyboard.

The most common 'Latin'-based keyboards are QWERTY but there also QWERTZ, AZERTY, and QZERTY. Computer keyboards are modified and sold with country-specific characters for ease of use.

People relocating overseas often decide to take favorite DVDs with them believing a DVD is a DVD. However, electronic entertainment discs such as DVDs and Blu-rays are coded and can only be played in the region they were purchased (US, Europe, Asia). In some locations it is possible to buy universal DVD players but check this out before spending serious money on unusable DVDs.

> **TIP**
> Inquire about your host country's electrical specifications and appliances before you ship your possessions abroad.

Office supplies

Most executives will admit their lives could not function as well as they do without their administrative assistants. While administrative personnel are invaluable, office supplies are an essential component of getting the work done, yet no one gives pencils, paper, or binders a second thought. Basic products do not have the same criteria, dimensions or standards worldwide.

- The business card does not have the same dimensions from country to country.
- An ISO* standard of paper is used internationally but is less common in the United States.
- Some countries file documents in three-ring binders while two-ring binders are more common in other places.

* International Organization of Standardization widely referred to as ISO

Food

People imagine when they purchase a food product they are familiar with it will have the same taste.

> The first time Australian, Mary, went to the cinema in Prague she bought refreshments at the concession counter - popcorn, M&M's® and a bottle of water. She sat down to enjoy the film and ate her first kernels of popcorn. It was not the lip-smacking flavor she was expecting, it was *sweet*. Now Mary liked sugar-coated popcorn but not when she was expecting the salty version.

What people are expecting and what they receive do not always match, even if the names are the same and they appear similar. The basic principles are applied, but the end product is created to serve the local population's taste and expectations. The unique aspects of ethnic food get lost when it is taken to another country. How dishes are prepared and the ingredients used impact the meals we are served and can help explain the inconsistencies. For example:

- Mexican food from Mexico is milder than the corresponding dishes prepared in New Mexico. New Mexicans love to add plenty of red or green chili.
- When ordering Chinese food in London's Chinatown notice how the local Chinese order and receive different dishes than their Western counterparts.
- Pizza may originate from Italy but each country adds its own local ingredients; the dough with topping retains the name but a sushi pizza, a barbeque chicken pizza and a margarita pizza are worlds apart.

Small variations in words, ingredients, and configurations can be the difference between brilliant and dreadful.

QUIZ – THE DEVIL'S IN THE DETAILS

1. There are how many regional codes for Blu-ray discs?
   a. None
   b. Three
   c. Six
   d. Ten

2. How many countries do not officially use the ISO 'A-series' paper.
   a. Two
   b. Four
   c. Eight
   d. Sixteen

3. Which executives of which merger spent countless hours discussing the size of their future business card?
   a. Alcatel-Lucent
   b. Exxon-Mobil
   c. Price-Waterhouse
   d. Daimler-Chrysler
   e. Glaxo-SmithKline

4. If a country uses 220v appliances, all of the plugs are interchangeable?
   a. True
   b. False

5. Creating streets and walkways with cobblestones is an old-fashion method of finishing road and pedestrian paths that hasn't been used since the 1960s.

   a. True
   b. False

6. Bed sizes are not universal. Match the queen-size bed measurements and the country.

Queen-size bed dimensions	Country
60x80 inches (152x203 cm)	Japan
60x80 inches (152x203 cm)	Australia
63x79 inches (160x200 cm)	Brazil
60x77 inches (152x196 cm)	Europe

May I Help You?

What is good customer service? The answer: it depends. The definition of good service is not universal and is measured using various parameters. While some consumers want and expect their every need to be met, even anticipated, other shoppers would find such attention intrusive, pushy and unpleasant. Consumers' expectations vary and stem from experience and commodities' value. A spectrum of service approaches is used in business:

- The customer is always right
- Ask and receive
- Experts know best
- Please let us serve you

The customer is always right

Some retailers and service providers embrace the philosophy that 'The Customer is Always Right' because they believe a happy consumer will be a long-term patron. This approach means sales staff are friendly and helpful, they tell the shopper what they want to hear and give them what they ask for, and if the purchaser is not satisfied with an item, it can be returned. Many businesses in the United States practice this ideology, but it is not effective in all countries.

Ask and you shall receive

Some shopkeepers like to let their patrons look around the store and make their selection. The shop staff are willing to answer questions but do not want to be too presumptuous about a customer's needs, they help the customer upon request. Many shops and department stores in Europe prefer to let the customer make the first move by asking for assistance.

Experts know best

Experts or specialists are frequently consulted for high-end goods or specialty services because clients want assurance they are getting their money's worth. Many store proprietors and restaurateurs believe they have expertise the client may not have, and believe customers should heed the professionals' advice and cautions. Major department stores, such as John Lewis in the UK and Nordstrom in the US provide personal shoppers and stylists, particularly in the clothes departments, to help you with your selections. Some professionals are renowned for their knowledge but it is accompanied by arrogance, such as temperamental chefs, who are famous for becoming irate if the patron requests a modification to their dishes.

> During the meal and wine selection for our wedding reception, which was to be held in a castle, I asked the coordinator to serve the coffee at the same time as the dessert, customary in the United States. He brusquely informed me that he was not going to tarnish his reputation to accommodate my request because coffee and tea are always served after dessert.

Please let us serve you

Owners or employees of market stands work in an extremely competitive environment, and actively attempt to garner the attention of potential customers. They strive to entice the potential consumers into their sales area, beseech passersby to interact with them and share what they are looking for and/or tempt them with a variety of bargains.

Similarly, restaurants in many tourist areas in Europe, North Africa and some parts of Asia try to cajole and charm prospective patrons into eating at their establishment. They have staff members, who stand outside with a menu, trying to persuade passersby to patronize their eating establishment.

Failure to understand the cultural implications can be costly

Satisfied customers usually mean happy merchants; however, understanding what the consumer wants is both a science and an art. Millions are spent annually on market research to collect information so company executives can make informed business decisions. The most successful firms take cultural differences into account. Understanding the expectations of potential clients is essential to conducting business in another country. What works in one place, may fail miserably in another.

> Tesco, a UK-based supermarket chain, the third largest retailer in the world, struggled when it entered the US market. Some customers described the interior as being more like a hospital than a grocery store and Tesco stopped the practice of using discount coupons, popular with many shoppers. Similarly, Carrefour was not successful in South Korea; the failure was attributed to not offering the 'right' product for the market and poor location choice.

> **TIP**
> **When selling across borders, selling in the local language is always more effective.**

QUIZ – MAY I HELP YOU

1. Match the company and one of its slogans:

Company	Slogan
Coca Cola	Just Do It
Mercedes Benz	Make Believe (2009)
Sony	Diamonds are Forever
Nike	The Best or Nothing (2010)
De Beers Consolidated Mines	It's the Real Thing (1971)

2. What company had to modify the design on its shoe because it offended some Islamic groups?

    a. Nike
    b. Adidas
    c. Puma
    d. New Balance
    e. Tiger

3. Some words have positive connotations in business, others negative. Put the following words in the proper category:

    Cheap   Inexpensive   Slick   Bargain   Haggle
    Expensive   High-end   Pricey   Sincere   Polished
                Smooth   Quibble   Negotiate

Positive	Negative

4. Match the idiom with its meaning:

Idiom	Meaning
A lemon	Buyer Beware
Beat about the bush	Agree to do something at a later date
A diamond in the rough	Important terms of an agreement which usually favor the seller over the buyer
Give Someone a 'rain check'	Poor quality product, usually an automobile
A pigeon	Something or person with potential, but needs a bit of work.
Fine print	Avoid answering question or concern
Caveat Emptor	The buyer needs to be responsible for checking the product or service is up to scratch

5. Match the material with the appropriate damage word.

Material	Damage
Metal/aluminum	Tarnish
Porcelain/China/Pottery	Dent
Leather	Tear, snag
Clothing	Crack, shatter
Silver, Bronze	Scuff

Domestic Goddess

Domestic chores are a part of everyday life and little thought is given that they may be done differently in other countries. Most people would prefer not to think about doing laundry, taking out the trash/rubbish or washing the car but knowing how these household responsibilities are accomplished can be helpful when living in another country.

Laundry

If a clean uniform or shirt is needed for school or work the next day, a load of laundry can easily be done in the United States, where the average wash cycle is about twenty minutes. Conversely, the cycle is closer to two hours in Western Europe. In Europe washing machines are modern; only delicate items are washed by hand. The difference is a result of the requirement for environmentally friendly machines using less water. Top-loaders are found in the United States, Canada, Australia, and Brazil while front-loaders are more common in Europe and the Middle East.

Laundry products also vary significantly:

- Detergents may be produced by the same manufacturer, but the brand names are rarely the same
- Multi-purpose spot cleaner versus 12-15 specific stain removers
- Liquid fabric softener versus dryer sheets

> When Shelia, a Brazilian, went to buy laundry detergent in Antwerp she did not find any brands she recognized so she picked one at random. Her expatriate friends sang the praises of the powerful soaps that removed hand-painted designs on T-shirts so she could not understand why her daughter's clothes never seemed to get clean. Sheila discovered after several months she had been using

a water softener to wash her clothes, not detergent. They are used to prevent chalk buildup and are sold in the same aisle as laundry detergent.

> **WATCH OUT!**
> **Check with your neighbors about hanging clothes outside to dry – it may be prohibited.**

Taking out the garbage/rubbish

Taking out the trash. Everyone has done it, yet no one particularly likes this messy, stinky chore. Western Europe has taken the task of trash removal and the process of recycling to a new level, driven by regulation and financial disincentives. For example, recycle fees are often paid at the time of purchase of 'white goods'. In some communities in Europe recycling is an art; they have as many as twelve separate containers, or curb-side pickups, each designated for a specific type of waste. Laurie, an expat living in Sweden, explained at a FAWCO regional meeting that some waste there is recycled for specific uses, for example food waste is converted to bio-gas to power local buses.

This dialogue between Theresa, living in Austria and her visiting cousin, Mark from Canada, illustrates differing perspectives on recycling.

Mark: Yes, recycling is good but you are fanatical about it.

Theresa: How can you say that? We just divide our trash and put it in designated containers.

Mark: You wash your garbage!

Theresa: We do not.

Mark: And what are you doing to that butter tub?

Theresa: Oh, I just hate to put in to the recycle bin greasy.

Mark: See you wash your trash!

Theresa: I guess that's how you see it.

Car wash

How clean a car is kept, inside and out, generally depends on the owner as well as the car. New cars, expensive models and sports vehicles tend to be cleaned more often. Some people choose to go to a car wash while others opt to do it themselves, or have their teenage child do it. Schools and clubs sometimes hold car washes to raise money.

> A large percentage of service stations in Germany have a small automatic car wash on the property. Not because Germans are fastidious and must have a clean car but because it is illegal to wash your car outside of designed areas, such as service stations. The law is intended to protect the water supply from pollutants, including oil or tar, which might wash off the vehicle and go into the sewer system.

Learn the laws

Whether it is throwing cigarette butts on the ground, paying for a grocery bag or buying garbage sacks from the local government authorities, knowing the expectations and laws associated with domestic chores in your host country is helpful. Did you know that both smoking and chewing gum in the street are illegal in Singapore?

TIP
Visit your local government office and ask about regulations, resources and garbage clearing schedules. Often they will have information for you printed in your own language.

QUIZ – DOMESTIC GODDESS

1. Instead of having a compost barrel in their garden some people keep a certain variety of bird in their garden, to help with the disposal of food scraps. What bird is kept?

    a. Chicken

    b. Pigeon

    c. Duck

    d. Goose

    e. Pheasant

2. What are other terms for 'domestic goddess'?

    a. Homemaker

    b. House woman

    c. Housekeeper

    d. Maid

    e. Wife

3. Many clothing manufacturers use symbols to provide washing instructions on clothing labels. Match the symbol with the advice:

Tumble dry   Dry clean   No bleach   Hand-wash   Iron on medium

    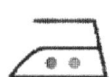 

_____   _____   _____   _____   _____

© copyright symbols by Ginetex

4. In European countries, on what type of items would this symbol most likely be found?

   a. Glass bottles
   b. Paper products
   c. Small appliances
   d. Plastic packaging and aluminum products
   e. Shoe boxes

5. Which of the following is **not** true?

   a. Hanging clothes outside on a clothes line to dry to save energy and to get fresh-smelling clothes is forbidden in some communities
   b. In some cities different colored garbage denote the type of rubbish disposed of
   c. In some localities, cars must be washed in a government operated car wash
   d. Glass is recycled by color in some countries

6. Which type of light bulb is being phased-out by some governments to encourage the use of newer technology and more efficient alternatives?

   a. Incandescent
   b. Neon
   c. Fluorescent
   d. Light-emitting diode (LED)

But It Was On Television

Most people trust their local news providers, but audiences do recognize one program may be more liberal than another. Generally the viewers want to believe they are getting the complete story. They want the truth, but facts by themselves can be boring and time constraints generally make it impossible for all of them to be presented. It is up to journalists, editors and other members of the media to decide what information to present. However, one fact can change an entire story and when details are withheld for brevity or sensationalism, determining the whole truth and nothing but the truth becomes virtually impossible.

News

Naturally, each country has its own television networks and associated news broadcasts that cater to their local market. Some of the networks such as CNN and BBC World are broadcast outside their home country and have an entirely different set of news broadcasters and programs. They have their own target audience; the programming is modified for another viewership. This was particularly evident when reporting on controversial topics:

- The war in Iraq
- The Middle East conflict

An American broadcast showed pictures of weapons confiscated on the West Bank, the BBC reported the story using the same photographs but added the weapons had been found in a police station in the West Bank. One fact can change the message.

The reporting also changes when country nationals are involved. Consider the following stories:

- The dalliances of IMF chairman, Dominique Strauss-Kahn – the reporting in France regarding events surrounding the accusations of rape did not resemble those reported by the US media
- Amanda Knox, charged with the murder of her roommate British student, Meredith Kercher – Amanda was portrayed as the 'girl next door' in the US, with a more sinister portrayal in the UK and Italy

> **TIP**
> **Read more than one account of a story in different media.**

Entertainment

Although every industrialized country creates local entertainment, the United States is still the largest (in terms of revenue) producer of motion pictures. Distribution of television programs and films to multiple countries is big business. Sometimes they are shown in their original version but often films and television programs are modified for the local audience by one of three methods: subtitles, voice over or dubbing.

Subtitles

Reading subtitles is a technique that needs to be practiced; the novice finds it difficult to read the texts fast enough. Programs on the television or in the theater are usually shown in their original version with subtitles.

> Canadian Ruth was thrilled about her husband's assignment to Belgium; she had read that programs were broadcast in their original format so there was no need to bring entertainment material on disc. Much to Ruth's surprise, when she arrived she found the shows that were dubbed were those for children.

> **WATCH OUT!**
> Nearly all countries dub programs for children especially for those too young to read subtitles. You may need to investigate purchasing a satellite dish or a Sling Box so you can watch your local television from back home.

Voice over

The original audio is reduced and local announcers translate the information. Although this technique is being used less and less for standard programming, it is used for live broadcasts.

Dubbing

Dubbing is the use of a new soundtrack with a translation of the original dialogue; some countries make considerable efforts to synchronize the translation and to select a voice comparable to the performer. Although for many viewers this is the preferred method, it is not without its challenges:

- One of the scenes in *Saving Private Ryan* involves the US soldiers struggling to communicate in French. As a French client noted, it wasn't the same when the film was shown in French.

> **TIP**
> When you are trying to learn a new language watching dubbed programs is a huge help because you hear the language spoken at a normal rate, the correct accent is used and you can expand your vocabulary as you read the local language subtitles.

QUIZ – BUT IT WAS ON TELEVISION

1. Which country produced the most films in 2011?

    a. China

    b. India

    c. Nigeria

    d. USA

    e. United Kingdom

2. What are the two major news networks frequently available in hotels and from many local senders?

    a. CNN and BBC World

    b. CNBC and CBS

    c. Bloomberg and HR News

    d. USA Today and The Herald

3. What media tycoon was disgraced by his media empire's unethical tactics in 2011?

    a. Ted Turner

    b. Oprah Winfrey

    c. Rupert Murdoch

    d. Martha Stewart

    e. Steve Forbes

4. On a television program about young people with money, the original dialogue said the young man would have no trouble attracting girls because he had a 'trust fund' but it was translated that the young man had a 'savings account'. Was this the best translation?

   a. Yes
   b. No

5. Which language technique is the primary method of modification used for works other than for children in the entertainment industry? Please write the correct word, 'dubbing' or 'subtitles' beside each country.

   Brazil   _____

   Croatia   _____

   Greece   _____

   Israel   _____

   Ukraine   _____

LIFESTYLES, ATTITUDES AND TRADITION

One Stop Shopping

Although some people only eat what they grow and/or raise, the majority of families purchase their food from stores, shops and markets. For the busy person doing all of their grocery shopping in one large supermarket is ideal, but others prefer to patronize specialty shops or markets. A few of the surprises you might encounter when you go grocery shopping in a new culture,

- Location
- Hours of Operation
- Packaging
- Seasonality

> **TIP**
> **Herbs and spices names are rarely in traditional translators or dual language dictionaries so look them up before heading to the store. Find out how the locals describe popular products so you know what to look for.**

Location

While modern supermarkets are continuing to multiply, offer convenience and everything under one roof, other fascinating options are available. Many towns around Europe, Asia and Africa have daily or weekly markets. Vendors sell their wares from stands, tents or specially designed trucks. Food abounds in these markets where barkers try to entice the next customer to buy their goods. Some farmers harvest their crops, sell most of it commercially but make a small amount available to the neighbors at roadside stands. Other growers have fields specifically set aside for visitors who want to pick or gather their own berries, pumpkins, and so on.

> Some farmers in Bavaria have flower fields on the edge of their farms for the neighborhood. They post the price per stem for sunflowers, tulips and gladiolas, provide knives for the cutting and a cashbox. It is an honor system respected by those who enjoy the tradition.

How food is displayed is important in some cultures, including Japan, but in other places it appears to be more a matter of function, getting the food out for the customer. Where items are shelved, their location within the store may seem logical in one country but not in another. While shopping, I have made a few observations:

- Greeting cards are displayed next to hair products
- Milk is kept in the soft drink aisle
- Baking soda is bought from a pharmacy
- Banking can be done at the post office
- Aspirin is not sold in mega-quantities

> **TIP**
> **Don't assume a product is not available – ask.**

Hours of Operation

Grocery shopping is an errand that has to be done. People from countries such as Russia, Brazil or Hong Kong, who are used to doing the task anytime of the day or night, any day of the week, get frustrated when stores are not open early mornings, evenings or both days on the weekend. In some countries, including Austria, many shops close over lunch in other countries. In Spain stores close in the afternoon from 2:00pm – 5:00pm (14:00-17:00) but are open again in the evening. It is not unusual for family owned restaurants and shops to close and post a sign indicating when they will return so they can take a family vacation. Many governments, particularly in Western Europe, regulate the number of hours a store can be open and the periods it must be closed.

Packaging

Using cans, jars or boxes for packaging can vary from country to country. It can be quite a surprise when you look for a can of soup and only find packages of dried, condensed soup, or if your recipe calls for vanilla bean but all you can find is vanilla extract. Countries where convenience is a priority are more likely to have all-in-one cake mixes and pre-packaged dinners, while other markets offer plenty of the basics so you can make your dessert from scratch. Some shoppers want the economy size that lasts for a month and other customers travel by foot or bike so they require smaller, more manageable containers. Whether it is vegetables in jars, cereals in bags or a 10 kg sack of flour, what is offered by the shops and/or demanded by the local residents is not consistent from country to country.

Seasonality

In some countries, such as the United States, stores import fruits and vegetables from around the world to ensure their customers have whatever produce they desire, when they want it. Availability of fresh berries or seasonal vegetables such as asparagus or squash in many places is limited to the period when the items are ripe and ready for harvest. Under Communist rule and in UN-sanctioned countries, only fruits and vegetable grown locally are in markets or on shop shelves.

> Gabrielle described why oranges were so special to her. She explained that living in the Czech Republic until the fall of Communism meant citrus fruits were rare. The family usually got one crate of oranges at Christmas time; they were a treasured treat.

Political climates influence food inventories and produce. The shelves might be full one day and empty the next. Working or living in a region of unrest means product availability is inconsistent.

> **TIP**
> **Learn from the locals – ask them for their own creative recipes for seasonal produce.**

QUIZ – ONE STOP SHOPPING

1. Match the fruit or vegetable and the major world producer:

Fruit and Vegetable	Country
Orange	Côte d'Ivoire
Apples	Canada
Olive	Spain
Pea	China
Cacao Bean	Brazil

2. Which country does not have more than 40% of their GDP in agriculture? (2010 data)

    a. Guatemala
    b. Liberia
    c. Chad
    d. Rwanda
    e. Tanzania

3. What is another name for baking soda?

    a. Baking power
    b. Allspice
    c. Sodium
    d. Sodium bicarbonate
    e. Yeast

4. Shopping – match the food group with the specialty shop:

Food Group	Specialty Shop
Pastries	Deli
Poultry, veal, sausage	Farmers Market
Fresh produce	Health Food Store
Corn Beef, Gouda, Gorgonzola	Butcher shop
Wheat germ, organic products	Bakery

5. Which is not a winter vegetable?

   a. Garlic
   b. Asparagus
   c. Fig
   d. Spinach
   e. Broad bean

6. Which is not a supermarket chain?

   a. Carrefour
   b. Foodsmart
   c. Aldi
   d. E-Mart
   e. Billa

The Grammar of Food

Nearly every language has words with the same or virtually identical pronunciation, words which have multiple definitions and two or more words with quite similar meanings. The same phenomenon can be applied to food. English actually has specific names for each word group.

- Homonyms = words that have the same pronunciation but different meanings (two goats/ go to the zoo)
- Homographs = words have the same spelling but different meanings (book a trip, read a book)
- Synonyms = words with identical meanings (to finish the work/ to complete the work)

These concepts can be applied to food.

Homonyms – Same name, different products

When a person is offered a truffle, their taste buds prepare for a particular flavor. For the food aficionado, the very expensive, relatively rare mushroom-type fungi might be what they are anticipating. A chocolate lover is imagining a chocolate confectionary filled with a ganache crème. While both are truffles, with their own attributes, their tastes are completely different.

The word '*Pannenkoek*' translates from Dutch to English as pancake but Dutch *pannenkoek* is prepared as a *crêpe* not as the fluffy, thicker US American pancake.

Homographs – Same products, different taste

Order milk, iced tea or doughnuts and you will receive a product that appears to be what you expect, but the taste can be very different. For example, the pasteurizing processes used to safeguard milk are not the same around the world. Many parts of Europe and countries like Australia and South Africa sell 'long-life' milk which can sit on a shelf for months rather than a week in a refrigerator.

> When Lucie and her husband began their expat life just out of college, one of the biggest hurdles they faced was their children's discerning taste buds. Their three children swore they could taste the difference in the milk. Although milk in both Belgium and Germany is pasteurized by the same method, her children swore they could taste a difference. Until her children were teenagers, she regularly hauled milk in large quantities to Germany.

Iced tea is a common refreshing drink available in many restaurants in the majority of European communities. What might be a surprise to some is that the iced tea is sweet and carbonated and not simply made by chilling previously brewed black tea.

Doughnut-type pastries are popular around the world but they are prepared, served and even named with a local twist. Some have a savory filling, others are filled with jelly and some may be filled with various flavored creams.

We have a taste in our mouth, an image in our mind or/and expectation when it comes to specific foods. When we are served a food that is not what we expected, we may be pleasantly surprised or very disappointed.

Synonyms – Same product, different names

Ouzo, the anise flavored liquor produced in Greece, is also known as Sambuca, Raki and Pastis originating from Spain, Turkey and France, respectively. Similarly, the British refer to two types of produce as the courgette or aubergine, which US Americans call zucchini and eggplant, respectively.

TIP
Food is one of the more challenging aspects of a new life for children. Do not say "yuck".

Exceptions

Language grammar always has some exceptions. Similarly, food is not consistent from place to place. One country's delicacy is another country's discarded scraps. Frequently what people eat is based on availability, tradition and preference. Additionally, consumption is affected by what the body can handle and is influenced by the foods they are accustomed to. Drinking water in some countries may be unhealthy for tourists/visitors because the water could contain bacteria, parasites or not have been purified; it usually poses little health risk to the locals, whose immune systems have developed a tolerance over time and exposure. Even if the nourishment does not present any health threats, certain food products still may not be enjoyed by non-locals.

- Vegemite – a spread for sandwiches, crackers and biscuits that originates from Australia. Has anyone ever met a non-Australian who liked the taste of Vegemite from the onset?
- Marzipan – a paste made from almonds. It is used in Europe to sweeten pastries, and candy is also made from it. European children and adults love it, most Americans cannot imagine why.
- Peanut butter – a spread produced from peanuts as the name suggests. Nearly every American child has taken a peanut butter and jelly sandwich to school at least once. Peanut sauces are popular in Indonesia and The Netherlands; these sauces were introduced to the Netherlands when Indonesia was a colony.
- Schmalz – a spread made from goose and pig fat. Bavarians spread it on pretzels and bread, non-Germans wonder why.

None of the above mentioned items are likely to make first-timers physically ill, nevertheless they are generally an acquired taste.

TIP
Try different foods, begin with small portions and always ask the local residents what they would suggest.

QUIZ – THE GRAMMAR OF FOOD

1. Match the name of the doughnut with the country.

Doughnut name	Country
Smoutebollen	Israel
Sufganiyot	Germany
Kreppel/Krapfen	Finland
Lihapiirakka	Belgium

2. Many of the same foods in the United Kingdom and the United States are not called the same thing. Match the foods.

United Kingdom	United States
Banger	Cupcake
Fairy cake	Dessert
Jelly	Ground beef
Minced meat	Sausage
Pudding	Jell-O (gelatin dessert)

3. 'Long-life' milk which is pasteurized using the ultra-high temperature treatment (UHT) technique extends the shelf-life of milk to_____, until it is opened?

   a. One – two months
   b. Six – eight weeks
   c. Three – four months
   d. Six – nine months
   e. One – two years

4. Steak Americain is also known as Steak Tartar?

    a. True
    b. False

5. What specially trained type of animal is used to find truffles in the forest?

    a. Pig
    b. German Shepherd
    c. Golden Retriever
    d. Siamese cat
    e. Ferret

6. Chocolate is chocolate! Oh dear, I know most chocolate enthusiasts will beg to differ. Match the chocolate with the country of origin.

Chocolate manufacturer	Country
Nestlé	Belgium
Neuhaus	Italy
Ferrero	Venezuela
Hershey	Switzerland
El Rey	United States

It's A Celebration!

Food is a focal point of most holiday celebrations, irrespective of country or religion, serving traditional foods such as Christmas goose or sweet baked treats for Chinese New Year. Frequently the dishes have special significance, having been passed down from generation to generation; family members will usually attest their version of traditional food tastes better than anyone else's.

> Claire was describing her Thanksgiving preparations and recited her menu. It included Grandmother Hudson's coconut cake, cousin Margaret's sweet potato/cranberry dish, cousin Patti's crunchy corn/calabacitas and a healthy green bean dish made by fitness-nut daughter, Amelia.

In Latin America the meal is prepared by one family and the extended family arrives to devour the feast. In other places, such as the US, the meal is described as a potluck and each family contributes a dish to the buffet table.

> **TIP**
> **Extending and accepting invitations for holiday celebrations are some of the best ways to gain insight into local customs and traditions.**

Since traditional celebration dishes are often only made once a year, it can be a rude awakening to realize that 'basic' ingredients in one country are not 'basic' in another. Individuals who have access to a store carrying the specialty items are very fortunate, but most of the time cooks must visit multiple stores, shop online and learn to improvise.

> Delia prefers to bring the ingredients she needs to prepare for her Chinese New Year parties from Hong Kong. She knows the food is authentic because the products are purchased in reliable shops she used to patronize. Her relocation to Munich has meant

visiting more stores, substituting ingredients and occasionally modifying her menu.

> **TIP**
> **If you have a celebration meal planned, plan your menu and acquire your ingredients in advance. If not, you may need a plan B.**

Bringing specialty items from your home country can be helpful, although importing fresh ingredients may not be practical. Some countries, such as Australia and the United States, have strict laws prohibiting the import of fresh products like fruit, vegetables, meats and cheeses.

> **WATCH OUT!**
> **Check the local import laws to prevent receiving a fine and having your food products confiscated.**

QUIZ – IT'S A CELEBRATION!

1. Match the number of public holidays with the country, but remember the number of paid holidays depends on the company, an employee's status in the firm and if the holiday falls on a weekend, the numbers can increase or decrease, accordingly.

Country	Public holidays
Egypt	11 days
Chile	16 days
Bosnia	12 days
Saudi Arabia	21 days
Russia	28 days

2. What one factor is most influential on holidays in nearly every country:

   a. Religion
   b. Country's history
   c. Hallmark greeting cards company
   d. Recognition of prominent individuals

3. Match the food and the country. These food items, which are rather typical in their home country might not be easily found around the world

Country	Food Item
United Kingdom	Cheese fondue
Germany	Christmas pudding
Switzerland	Vindaloo sauce
India	Osechi-ryori
Japan	Knoedel

4. What are Christmas crackers?

   a. Appetizer made with crackers, slices of cheddar cheese and topped with green olives or red pimento
   b. Sweet biscuits
   c. Ornaments hung on the Christmas tree
   d. Table decorations that contain a surprise and are pulled apart with a 'bang'

5. After which religious period is the *Eid al-Fitr* held? It is referred to as the 'Sugar Festival' in Turkey

   a. Carnival
   b. Lent
   c. Ramadan
   d. Passover

6. At which holiday meal are jelly/jam doughnuts served?

   a. Easter
   b. Hanukah
   c. Chinese New Year
   d. All Independence Day celebrations

Polite or Rude? That is the Question

William of Wykeham (1324-1404), Bishop of Winchester and Chancellor of England, is credited with saying, "Manners maketh the man" but as modern-day cultural expert, Richard Lewis writes, "Cross-culturally, they can unmaketh him as well".

'Please', 'Thank you' – basic courteous words most people learn to use as children, become ingrained. Every language uses polite terms, nevertheless what constitutes good manners is not universal.

> Paul walked into the home of American friends of mine, whom he had never met. Our hostess, Anna said, "Mark is at the grill. Paul, grab a beer from the cooler and join him." Paul glanced at me and I nodded that yes, he needed to 'help himself' to a beer and join Mark outside. Reluctantly Paul did just that, although it was counter to what he had been taught were good manners.

US Americans want guests to be comfortable in their home so they encourage a more casual atmosphere, steering away from formality. To 'make yourself at home' means you are part of the family, you are therefore welcome in the kitchen. You will probably hear 'help yourself' and it would not be unusual to be encouraged to open the refrigerator or a cupboard. Conversely, these same behaviors could be seen as unacceptable in much of Western Europe.

This section will highlight three aspects of table manners:

- Hands at the table
- Handling cutlery
- Honored guest
- Expressing gratitude or satisfaction

Hands at the table

Should hands be placed on the table or in the lap and what about forearms and elbows? Placement of the hands cannot be ignored because it is not a gesture that goes unnoticed. Interestingly, the napkin usually follows the hands so if the hands are in the lap so is the napkin and vice versa.

> **TIP**
> **Watch others at the table and follow suit.**

Handling cutlery

Cutlery is common in Europe, the Americas, Australia and parts of Asia and Africa. There are a plethora of forks, knives and spoons but no universal agreement on their specific use. Italians believe pasta should be eaten with a fork (no spoon support and do not cut it up), some British flip their fork upside down for their peas, and in the US a knife is for cutting a single bite, while using both a fork and knife at the same time is common in much of Europe. Chopsticks are preferred in many Asian countries and in many places in Africa, bread-type foods, such as chapattis, are the primary tool for eating.

> While visiting Ann in Washington DC we chose an African restaurant. We ordered several dishes to share which were served with flat tortilla type bread. The bread was our utensil for scooping and eating the food. What I did not know at the time was we probably should have only used our right hands.

The left hand is considered dirty by most Muslims; consequently, food should not be eaten with it and items should not be passed with the left hand either.

> **TIP**
> **While using local utensils may seem fun, be careful that you do not end up wearing your dinner.**

Honored guest

Being the guest of honor has its privileges but it isn't without its challenges. The important guest is seated in the place of honor and is served the best dish or part of the dish.

> During one of her first business trips to Japan, Magdalena was seated in what she described as a dark corner. At first she thought it was because she was a woman, only later she learned it was the place farthest from the door, therefore the highest place of honor.

Camiel tells the story of one of his early visits to China in which he was the senior member of the visiting team; consequently, he was served the 'best part' of the fish, the eyeballs. Although Camiel will attest they are not his favorite, he consumed them out of respect for his host.

> **TIP**
> **Being aware of country specialties can enable guests to be prepared for the food they will receive.**

Expressing gratification or satisfaction

Being hosted to a meal is a privilege, expressing delight and satisfaction is considered well-mannered and reasonable in any culture. The way in which this is accomplished varies markedly among cultures. Similar to gestures, getting it wrong may not be just an embarrassing blunder but actually very offensive.

> **WATCH OUT!**
> **Actions usually speak louder than words; knowing what will signal appreciation and what will offend your hosts is advisable.**

QUIZ – POLITE OR RUDE? THAT IS THE QUESTION

1. Two reasons are generally cited as the basis for people keeping their hands visible (on the table).

    a. Keeps the clothes clean and both hands are used for eating anyway
    b. Keeps the clothes clean and ensures there are no weapons at the table
    c. Reduces romantic activities under the table and ensures there are no weapons at the table
    d. Reduces romantic activities under the table and both hands are used for eating anyway

2. What food is not commonly eaten with the hands in the USA?

    a. Corn on the cob
    b. French fries
    c. Pizza
    d. Fried chicken
    e. Chili

3. A person should begin to eat as soon as they are served because otherwise the food may get cold

    a. True
    b. False

4. Where is burping a compliment to the host/hostess?

    a. Japan
    b. Korea
    c. Thailand
    d. Hong Kong
    e. All of the above

5. Leaving food on your plate – place the countries under the correct category.

   Russia   Sweden   USA   India   Mexico   Korea   Turkey
   Greece   Vietnam   South Africa

Leaving food on your plate is fine/good	Leaving food on your plate is negative

6. When there are multiple sets of flatware/cutlery on the table, which one(s) are used first?

   a. Begin with the flatware/cutlery on either side of the plate but that is closest to the plate

   b. Begin with the flatware/cutlery on either side of the plate but farthest from the plate

   c. It really does not matter, make your own choice

7. Match the place of honor at a table and the country:

Place of Honor	Country
Away from the door	Greece
To the right of the host	Japan
At the end of the table	United States
Middle of the table	Romania

Cheers!

A toast is a nice way to start a meal, especially if you have something to celebrate; a wedding, an accomplishment or a business deal. However, toasting varies considerably from country to country. Raising a glass is an area fraught with potential problems and you need to know:

- whether toasting is ever rude
- who initiates the toast
- how important is eye contact
- who pours the drink
- whether each individual glass must touch
- when the glass can be set down
- what word or phrase should be used when you raise the glass

In some countries guests should not begin to drink until after the host/hostess has offered a toast, in other countries toasting may be viewed as rude.

> Andrea was asked if it was true that Hungarians found toasting rude. Andrea, a Hungarian teacher, explained to the group that toasting with beer is considered rude, because during WWII their invaders toasted with beer during the execution of Hungarians.

As alcohol is seldom served in Muslim countries, toasting is rare. In other countries raising a glass to yourself is seen as arrogant. In Sweden men should not set their glasses down until all of the women have done so. Toasting has a long tradition in Asian countries but each has its own variation. In Korea a person is expected to empty their glass after a toast and at family feasts the glass is passed to the person on the right. In Japan a person's glass should never be empty.

Coca-Cola CEO, Muhtar Kent, made a toast to a group of business leaders and visiting dignitaries from a Chinese delegation, which included President Hu. While he attempted to be gracious by toasting in Chinese, he actually used the Japanese term '*kanpai*' meaning 'toast' or 'cheers' instead of the Chinese word '*ganbei*' which translates as 'dry glass'.

The effort and intention were good, but they were lost in the delivery. This faux pas did not cause any long-term damage to the relationship, but neither did it create the goodwill he had hoped.

In many countries and cultures drinking together is a time to get to know one another, for people to be a bit less self-conscious and/or to build relationships. Toasting is an integral component of these activities.

> **TIP**
> **If you do not drink alcohol, decline graciously and offer a brief explanation.**

QUIZ – CHEERS!

1. Match the toast with the corresponding country:

Toast	Country
Zum Wohl	Spain
Saude	Poland
Ganbei	Germany
Salud	Brazil
Stolat	China

2. Which of the following is not a common meaning for a toast?
   a. To your health
   b. Bottoms-up
   c. To enjoyment
   d. To us

3. Why don't US Navy personnel toast with water?
   a. They believe their ship will sink
   b. They believe it dooms the person being toasted to a watery grave
   c. They believe they will get sick
   d. They believe toasting with water is disrespectful

4. Match the toasting custom with the country:

Toasting Custom	Country
Drink only after the first toast is offered	Sweden
The glass is emptied, the last few drops are shaken out, then the host refills the glass	Russia
Make eye contact with every person you are toasting	USA
The guest of honor is toasted and should reciprocate	Middle East
Toasting is rarely done	Korea

5. Champagne is a commonly used to toast, sometimes sparkling wine is chosen as an alternative. Which is not a sparkling wine?
   a. Pastis
   b. Sekt
   c. Prosecco
   d. Cava
   e. Spumante

6. In many countries toasting yourself is not done, why?
   a. It is as though you are applauding yourself (conceited)
   b. It is considered bad luck
   c You will get sick
   d. It is considered disrespectful

7. What is a teetotaler?
   a. A tea lover
   b. Someone who grows tea
   c. Someone who does not drink alcohol
   d. A tea kettle maker
   e. A still for making alcohol

Babies, Weddings and Funerals

Families around the world celebrate rites of passage; the birth of a child, honoring a newly married couple and mourning the passing of loved ones. They serve to illustrate how connected we are, regardless of cultural background or country of origin. However, people observe these major events in different ways. Activities, whether religious or more secular, are steeped in tradition. Even if the celebrations are personal, the events frequently touch many lives. Since rituals play an important role in these rites, knowing the local practices is essential. The possibility for error is great,

- Gifts – type and when given
- Celebration/Recognition – invitations (how and who), when, where, how long
- Color – what is or is not appropriate
- Flowers – what is or is not acceptable
- Work – impact on job and colleagues
- Friends and family – expectations

Ruth, a UK transplant to Belgium, invited family and friends to her 50th birthday party. Some of her Belgian friends were a bit nervous about attending; they had never been invited to a 'family' celebration other than that of their own relatives.

> **WATCH OUT!**
> **When the family is abundant and nearby, friends and colleagues may be excluded from events – it is not personal, just tradition.**

Let's just look at the beginning and end of life.

Births

The arrival of a new member of the family is usually a happy occasion but also a time of adjustment. *The Unofficial Guide to Having a Baby,* by Ann Douglas and John R. Sussman, MD, for prospective parents, noted the reason newborns do not sleep the first few months after being born is they want their parents not to forget that their lives will never be the same again! Some countries, such as Norway, have very liberal family laws which allow one or both parents to spend months or years with their child with financial support and the ability to return to work, while other countries have no provisions.

In some places Baby Showers are given for the expectant parents to help them acquire items needed for the baby, in other regions a celebration before the baby is born is viewed as bad luck. In *Multicultural Manners,* by Norine Dresser, there is a story of a young Vietnamese woman who refused to look at her child in the hospital, believing it would bring the evil eye onto her baby. This highlights the different ways of expressing parental love to a newborn. Ignoring a newborn and not bonding with it is unthinkable in many cultures, but in parts of Asia calling attention to a young child is believed to bring negative consequences.

TIP
Expatriates should include other expats and new friends in their special events when their family is far away.

Death

Frequently religion dictates customary rituals; how quickly someone should be laid to rest, the acceptable methods of caring for remains of the deceased and the ceremonies conducted. In some cultures the events associated with the funeral are very subdued, but in others it can be seen as a celebration of a life. An Irish wake is a time to toast the deceased, share stories about his/her life, laugh and cry.

Black is a traditional color of mourning in many countries including Thailand, Japan, Tonga, Europe and the USA. Widows in some cultures continue to wear black for the rest of their lives. White is the color associated with death in India, China, and Cambodia. In South Africa red is associated with mourning.

Colors do not convey the same meaning across cultures, nor do flowers. The chrysanthemum is the symbol of the ruling family in Japan and Chrysanthemum Day is celebrated annually on the 9 September. Chrysanthemums are popular in the US and given as corsages during football season. Many countries see the chrysanthemum as a flower of happiness, however this is not always the case, so be sure to check before making a faux pas.

> Shortly after arriving in Belgium as a new bride, Rozanne, decided to brighten up the yard and impress her new family with a bit of gardening. She purchased thirty plants of 'mums, in all her favorite fall colors and proceeded to plant them all in the front garden. Her Belgian husband didn't say anything other than, "Nice work". Two weeks later it was 1 November, All Saints Day, a day to remember those who have passed away. Rozanne was surprised when they visited the local cemetery to find a sea of 'mums. Her husband confirmed this is the only place a person would find chrysanthemums in Belgium. This explained the strange looks Rozanne had gotten from the neighbors. A lovely rose garden now fills her flowerbeds.

TIP
Ask your local florist about appropriate flowers for funerals or other occasions.

QUIZ – BABIES, WEDDINGS, FUNERALS

1. In many parts of Europe including the Netherlands and Germany, who brings the birthday cake to the place of business?

    a. The boss

    b. A co-worker/colleague

    c. Birthday man/woman (person having the birthday)

    d. Family member

    e. No birthday cakes at work

2. Chrysanthemums come in many different varieties and colors but they also convey distinctive messages around the world. Match the message with the country.

Message	Country
Put at grave site on November 1st	United States
Used to create corsages particularly for school events	Japan
Royal flower, given on special occasions	Belgium

3. Paid Parental Leave is mandatory in many countries; one or both parents are allowed and sometimes required to take time off from their job to bond with the newborn and the time off is paid. Match the parental paid leave with the countries.

Parental Paid Days	Countries
Zero	Mexico, Ghana, Nigeria
90 days	Chile, Cuba
12 weeks	United States, Swaziland
18 weeks	Germany, Norway, Sweden
More than 1 year	China, Korea, Thailand

4. In which country does a woman not need her father's permission to marry?
   a. Saudi Arabia
   b. India
   c. Indonesia
   d. Bulgaria

5. Match the wedding custom with the region or country.

Wedding Custom	Country
Bride wears hues of red	UAE
Separate receptions for men and women	Zulu tribe in South Africa
Wedding cake is a fruitcake	Europe
Wedding rings worn on right hand	Scotland
Women only wore tops after marriage	India

6. In which country do babies receive diaper pins with a glass eye attached, which is intended to protect the child from evil wishes?
   a. Russia
   b. Philippines
   c. Turkey
   d. Nicaragua
   e. Nigeria

7. Newborns are precious – which of the following is **not** viewed as potentially bad luck in some cultures:
   a. Setting up the baby's room before the baby is born
   b. Holding a party for the expectant parents
   c. Complimenting the newborn
   d. Feeding the baby formula
   e. Showing the newborn to friends and extended relatives within the first 40 days

Hats Off to You

Gwyneth Olofsson, author of *When in Rome or Rio or Riyadh . . .* reminds us that how we dress is more than individual taste, and clothing is an integral part of a culture. Attire customary in one country may not be appropriate in another, and occasionally the outfit may be unlawful. The clothes someone wears may be a reflection of their personality and personal style, however there are outside factors which can influence a person's choice including climate, dress codes or customs.

Bridget and her boyfriend had stood in line for more than an hour waiting to enter St. Peter's Basilica in Rome. As they approached the entrance they were stopped, the church's staff explained that Bridget could not proceed into the Basilica because her shorts did not cover her knees. Many churches and temples require shoulders and/or knees to be covered before entering.

> **TIP**
> **In the summer when it is warm and you are dressed for the weather, carry a scarf with you that can function as a skirt or a shawl just in case.**

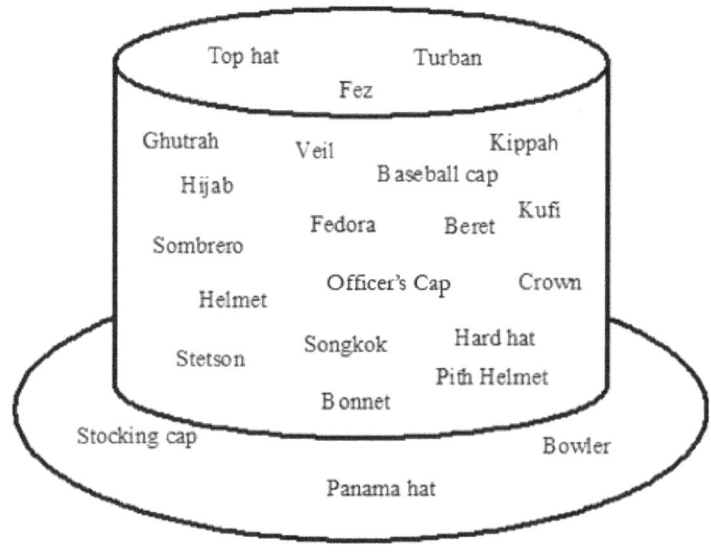

Take the hat, for example. It is practical for a daytime stroll along La Promenade des Anglais on the Mediterranean coast. Fifty years ago men and women who covered their heads with hats were commonplace in many cultures. Nowadays, people in many Western cultures primarily cover their head for practical reasons: protection, occupational requirements or to show respect. However hats and hairstyles still play an essential role in some cultures or religious groups. Here is a sampling of headwear, how many do you recognize?

Show respect

Many religions expect their faithful followers to cover their head all or some of the time. Most religious groups have very distinctive headwear; consider the *kippah* worn by Jewish men and the mantilla, a lace veil, worn to church by many women of Latin countries.

The *hijab*, worn by some Islamic women is fascinating because it takes on the style of the wearer. When several generations of women are seen together usually the grandmother has the longest, loose fitting *hijab*, her daughter wears a shorter, more expensive, but still conservative head scarf, and the granddaughter may have the *hijab* tightly wrapped around her head to show the bun in her hair. Sometimes the *hijab* is worn with a *burka* (the head to toe dark cloak) but other times with 'modern' clothing.

WATCH OUT!
Heads may be covered for religious reasons – asking someone to remove their head covering can be seen as confrontational or offensive.

Hairstyles

The way hair is worn/styled can also reflect a region or a religious group. Religious affiliation is often obvious by the hairstyle of devout believers. Many Buddhist monks shave their heads, Orthodox Jewish men do not shave their beards and wear 'sidelocks' and Sikh men do not shave facial hair or cut their hair. Tribal membership can influence how a member styles his/her hair, from braids to extensions, and from shaved heads to tattooed ones.

Touching the head

Patting a child on the head might be intended to be a sign of affection but often the gesture is not interpreted that way. Adults might find it condescending and some cultures in southeastern Asian would be mortified. These cultures believe that their spirit/soul resides in the head, it is sacred so touching it is not acceptable.

QUIZ – HATS OFF TO YOU

1. Why might Chinese men be embarrassed to wear a green hat?

    a. It tells everyone they are rich
    b. It indicates they are jealous of other family members
    c. It implies they are cheating on their spouse
    d. It signifies that they are part Irish

2. Match the idiom to the meaning:

Idiom	Meaning
Throw one's hat in the ring	Annoyed
Hat's off to you	Very quickly
At the drop of a hat	Equal
A bee in their bonnet	Indicate interest in something
To be head to head	Indicates admiration for someone

3. At what event do the hats worn by the women receive nearly as much attention as the sporting event itself?

    a. World Cup
    b. Super Bowl
    c. Ascot
    d. Wimbledon

4. Match the headwear with the explanation:

Headwear	Explanation
Stetson	Worn skiing
Songkok	Worn by some military & French
Stocking cap	Worn by Muslin men in Indonesia, Brunei, Malaysia, Singapore, the southern Philippines and southern Thailand,
Kufi	Another name for a cowboy hat
Beret	Originates from Africa

5. In Western cultures men are expected to remove their hat when they enter a building especially a church or someone's home

    a. True
    b. False

6. Female members of which religious group shave their heads?

    a. Hindu
    b. Orthodox Judaism
    c. Greek Orthodox
    d. Jehovah's Witness

Naked or Nude?

The statue of David by Michelangelo. Is he naked or nude? For some the distinction between the two words is minute and neither belongs in public; attitudes about decency vary considerably from culture to culture. Some societies and individuals have standards regarding what they believe is appropriate in their community. Norine Dresser, author of *Multicultural Manners*, is a proponent of tolerance and understanding regarding cultural divergence, particularly when they are based on religious belief or tenets such as modesty. Three areas will be highlighted:

- Public displays of affection
- Spas, pools and beaches
- Arts and media

Public Displays of Affection (PDA)

Some 'love-birds' are very affectionate in public, other couples in love believe affection should be expressed in private.

> As American, Douglas, prepared for his visit to meet the family of his fiancée, Pheng, he commented they were going to have to change how they interacted. They usually walked hand-in-hand, touched each other's face during private conversations and kissed when they went their separate ways. She noted they should respect the local customs and refrain from public displays of affection (PDA) which might be seen as too liberal in Indonesia.

Religious organizations and schools often establish rules regarding public displays of affection, or behavior such as dancing and frequently have guidelines as to how close or suggestive such contact might be. Opinions related to acceptability are usually a matter of age and experience; young people are often more liberal than older generations.

Europeans and South Americans are the most broad-minded on the topics of nudity, sex and free expression. Although being affectionate in public is not banned, some cultures in Asia believe affection should be demonstrated privately. PDA is illegal in most Islamic countries. Where would you put yourself on the spectrum of activities in public? What is allowed in your country?

Spas, pools and beaches

For centuries people have believed in the curative value of mineral water, particularly in Europe and Japan. Spas and communal bathhouses are places to access these healthy waters, however wearing swimwear there is considered unhygienic. Saunas are always taken naked in Finland. In some countries the facilities are separated by gender but not always.

> **WATCH OUT!**
> **You may find that swimwear is either not permitted or may not be obligatory in the sauna at a health spa.**

Public beaches have few restrictions in Europe and some parts of South America, consequently it is not unusual to find topless sunbathers and swimmers. A person certainly does not have to wear less than she/he is comfortable with, but try not to be shocked if this is not something you are used to in your own culture.

While nude beaches and camping facilities are available in Europe, they primarily cater to naturists. Baring it all is generally limited to designated areas, but the same restrictions do not apply to young children who may wear nothing on the beach.

Germans, Brigitta and Robert, recounted the story of taking their two-year-old daughter, Yasmin, to a beach in Florida. As they had done in Spain, they let her play in the water without a swim suit. Almost immediately, other beachgoers admonished them and demanded they clothe their child. While Brigitta and Robert did so, they won't forget the reaction their behavior caused; they assumed the same attitudes to nudity in Spain would apply to Florida.

Art and media

Each country has guidelines for its media, outlining what is acceptable or appropriate. Sometimes more mature material is relegated to a later timeslot, other times it is only available upon purchase and occasionally material with nudity and/or sexually explicit content is forbidden. In most of Europe varying degrees of nudity are used in advertisements, both in print and commercials. News coverage, which may include people in different stages of undress are broadcast and nothing is censored. Some Americans may have thought that the British were puritanical, but this is far from true – consider 'Page 3 Girls'.

> The British tabloid, *The Sun*, has featured topless or photos of scantily-clad women on page three since 1970, creating the term 'Page 3 Girls'.

Inhibitions about the human body are less common outside of the United States and the Middle East. In the Middle East foreign newspapers are censored with black marker pens – all exposed flesh is covered before publications are allowed to go on sale.

> **TIP**
> **When living or traveling in another country, you do not have to join in with the nakedness around you, but refrain from eye-rolling or 'tsking' like Grandma used to do.**

QUIZ — NAKED OR NUDE?

1. If a person is described by either one of two terms are they likely to be arrested for being naked?

    a. Nudist
    b. Naturalist
    c. Exhibitionist
    d. Streaker

2. Which religious group generally wants its members to be treated by medical physicians of the same gender?

    a. Buddhism
    b. Hinduism
    c. Judaism
    d. Islamic
    e. Christianity

3. The term Spa is said to originate from Spa, Belgium. Who named the city?

    a. The Romans
    b. The Greeks
    c. The British
    d. The Moors
    e. The Germans

4. Which country is not known for its communal bathhouses?

    a. Germany
    b. Turkey
    c. Romania
    d. Japan
    e. They are all known for their public bath houses

5. Which American singer created a scandal with a costume 'malfunction' in which one breast was momentarily visible on US television?

    a. Lady Gaga
    b. Janet Jackson
    c. Christina Aguilera
    d. Shakira
    e. Beyonce

6. Where would public displays of affection be a problem?

    a. Parts of Thailand
    b. Most Northern African countries
    c. Indonesia
    d. Cambodia
    e. All of the above

Luck of the Irish

Lucky at cards, unlucky in love. Is it true people can't have both love and money? Some individuals and cultures are superstitious; there are some who think it is nonsense and even those who may not appear to be superstitious would prefer not to tempt fate. People's actions will change if they believe luck is involved, good or bad. Superstitions tend to surface at stressful times or when someone is looking for an explanation or blame for good luck or misfortune.

Numbers

US Americans don't really trust the number 13 - add Friday to it and some people will stay home from work; conversely they love lucky number 7. Armenians think odd numbers are better than even ones, which are linked to death; similarly both Chinese and Japanese associate death and bad luck with the number 4. Skyscrapers in the United States rarely have a thirteenth floor and it is unlikely that buildings in Hong Kong or Taiwan would have a fourth floor; there are enough guests who would refuse to stay or work on them.

> Some municipalities in the USA with a large local Chinese population have had to establish processes and fees for address changes due to the number of requests received from residents who want to change their address to a more favorable number.

Flowers

Many Germans believe flowers received during a stay in a hospital should remain there otherwise the person will have a relapse and return to the hospital. A four-leafed clover or shamrock is believed to bring luck to the Irish. Receiving a dozen red roses is a sign of love to some but as mentioned above, an even number could be considered bad luck in some cultures.

A yellow bloom might signify 'let's be friends', but in Iran or Peru it tells the receiver they are hated. Many brides choose white flowers for their bouquets, but in China and many Asian countries this color is associated with death

> **TIP**
> Ask the local Florist for suggestions. They will know what is culturally appropriate.

Feng shui

Feng shui originates from China and some of the concepts have been adopted by individuals from other cultures. Feng shui is a practice believing that the site, structure and design of a building can influence the harmony of its inhabitants. Feng shui experts explain how the direction doors face, whether there are openings, whether windows and doors across from each other, and the placement of individual items within your house or office, can affect the energy in the building.

Tradition

Some Africans consult medicine men, witch doctors or women with mystical powers for advice. The Polterabend, a tradition in parts of Germany, is held an evening before the wedding of a couple when dishes are broken to bring the pair good luck; the couple-to-be also clean up the floor together as a sign of cooperation. Likewise a glass is stomped on at a Jewish wedding for good luck. Food is placed on small shrines in Thailand to keep the gods happy, which in turn blesses the family. Vietnamese and Turkish families have concerns about the evil eye coming onto their child, so take measures to ensure their newborns remain safe during their early lives.

> **TIP**
> What makes something good luck or bad luck is not always clear or rational but the beliefs can be strong and should not be ignored.

QUIZ – LUCK OF THE IRISH

1. Which company consulted Feng Shui experts before building their facility in Hong Kong to help ensure the business would be a success?

    a. Disney
    b. Six Flags
    c. McDonalds
    d. Crate & Barrel
    e. Century 21

2. Which of the following does **not** bring good luck?

    a. Cricket
    b. Horseshoe
    c. Chimney sweep
    d. Dog
    e. Elephants

3. Which of the following is bad luck?

    a. Giving a knife to a business associate
    b. Breaking a mirror
    c. A black cat
    d. Bathing or showering on New Year's Day
    e. All of these can bring bad luck

4. Match the country and the item which symbolizes good luck:

Country	Good Luck
Germany	Red Envelope
Ireland	Pig
China	Shamrock
Italy	Sapphire
India	Fish

5. Red flowers would be welcomed in China but in what country are they negative?

    a. Mexico
    b. United States
    c. Ghana
    d. Cambodia
    e. Bosnia

6. Match the national flower with the country:

National Flower	Country
Lotus	Costa Rica
Daffodil	Egypt
A blue water lily - *Nil Manel*	Jordan
An orchid - *guaria morada*	Sri Lanka
Black Iris	Wales

Man's Best Friend

'Animal lovers', 'dog lovers', 'cat lovers' are common phrases because so many people around the world love or honor animals.

Quarantine

Pet owners rarely want to leave their family pets behind if they relocate. Some countries require documentation related to the animal's health but there are countries including Australia, New Zealand and Japan which have very strict laws and even require the quarantine of an animal before it can enter the country.

> **WATCH OUT!**
> **Non-exotic pets accompanying the family on an international move is rarely an issue, but you need to prepare for a move three to six months before you leave to ensure your pet's paperwork and vaccinations are in order.**

What's its name?

The names people choose for their pets may reflect the color or personality of the animal, such as Blackie or Spirit, but this is not an option in countries that have laws on the naming of pure-breed dogs. Here are a couple of country examples:

Nicaragua = one letter of the alphabet per litter
France = a new letter of the alphabet each year, in 2012 it was 'H'
Brazil = names cannot be longer than 30 characters

The quality of life an animal's life varies tremendously from place to place. In some it may be:

- Sacred
- Welcome
- Outcast

Sacred

Hinduism is the third largest religion in the world and more than 80% of its followers reside in India. The sacredness of cows by Hindus is fairly well-known. Due to their status in India these animals have few restrictions so roam untethered through streets and public areas. While slow traffic can be anticipated based on the time of the day and public transportation schedules, there is nothing to predict the whim of a cow. It is particularly exasperating for visitors who are unaccustomed to having traffic jams caused by cows on the roads of a city such as New Delhi.

Welcome

Europeans appear to be animal lovers and while the naming rules are quite restrictive in some cases, zoning laws are much more lax. Farm animals such as sheep, chickens and horses as well as deer can be found in suburban neighborhoods and surrounding communities not specifically zoned for agriculture.

> In Flanders, in non-agriculture neighborhoods, families keep animals in their yards. In one such neighborhood several families have chickens, another has two horses, a sheep lives down the street and yes, another neighbor has eight deer.

It is very common in Western Europe to see dogs accompanying their owners for walks. Although dogs are frequently restricted entry from grocery stores they are generally allowed in most other stores. While there are those people who allow their dogs to sit on a chair or bench, the majority of dogs sit under or near the table. Again, there are exceptions but most of the dogs are well-behaved, often more well-mannered than some children.

Outcast

Some dogs are renowned for their aggressive nature, such as pit bulls and Rottweilers. People uncomfortable around dogs make an effort to keep their distance from bigger or aggressive behaving dogs. Not all cultures see pets as a good thing and may have a particular issue with one. Dogs are generally seen as dirty in Muslim countries therefore dogs are used for farm work or hunting but not kept as indoor pets. Consequently, many Muslim children are taught to avoid dogs so you may see children who appear apprehensive and take a wider circle around the dog you are walking; appreciate not everyone is the dog lover you are.

QUIZ – MAN'S BEST FRIEND

1. Which animal was revered by the Egyptians and causing its death meant death to the perpetrator?

    a. Dog
    b. Cat
    c. Rabbit
    d. Snake
    e. Camel

2. If someone is said to have 'a dog's life', what does that mean?

    a. an unhappy existence
    b. a great life
    c. a life of hard work
    d. a life with a big family

3. Which canine or feline diseases are countries worried about importing?

    a. canine distemper
    b. rabies
    c. canine parvovirus
    d. feline leukemia
    e. cancer

4. According to the Worldwatch Institute, in 2010 how much money was spent on pet food in the United States and Europe?

   a. $7 billion
   b. $17 billion
   c. $28 billion
   d. $37 billion
   e. $45 billion

5. Followers of which religion avoid actions which could harm or kill another living thing including walking in grass where there might be ants?

   a. Jehovah's witness
   b. Atheist
   c. Jainism
   d. Scientology
   e. Hare Krishna (International Society for Krishna Consciousness)

This Is So Taxing

Americans say there are only two certainties in life: death and taxes. Vast assortments of taxes are collected from individuals and companies by governments around the world. The list of levies below is by no means an exhaustive inventory but some of the more well known are:

- Sales tax
- Tourist tax
- Community tax
- Property tax
- Inheritance tax
- Income tax
- Self-employment tax
- Numerous corporate taxes

Sales tax

The rates and transparency of sales and tourist taxes annoys many shoppers. Hungary's Value Added Tax (VAT) is the highest in the world at 27%, but it is usually included in the price listed on a price tag/sticker. It can be quite frustrating for a shopper to be told at the cash register that the $20 price they thought they would be charged excluded sales tax. Airline fares have been notorious for leading potential passengers to believe they had found a great price only to realize the price did not include the taxes and fees. Hotels, particularly in tourist cities such as Rome, charge an additional tourist taxes (€1-3/person/night as of January 1, 2011).

> **WATCH OUT!**
> Always read the fine print and check about sales, tourist and other taxes before you commit to a purchase.

While tax avoidance is a national pastime in some parts of the world, most US Americans are wary of tax authorities, perhaps because it was tax evasion that ended the criminal reign of the likes of Al Capone, a notorious gangster from the 1920s.

Income tax

Tax laws are complex, cumbersome and fluid, attempting to navigate them without professional assistance is hazardous because the repercussions from mistakes can be expensive. Not having the knowledge or understanding of tax laws is no defense! Frequently, expatriate contracts include a provision for a tax advisor or tax assistance, but for a large percentage of individuals living outside their home country, the need for professional help is not recognized but is vital.

> As Karen was finishing graduate school in the United States she met her future Belgian husband, Luc. They married and Karen relocated to Belgium, learned Flemish and found a job. Karen paid her standard Belgian income taxes, nearly 50%, and everything was fine until her American friend, Ethan, made a comment about filing US taxes. Karen found his comment strange. Ethan explained that even though a specified amount of foreign income is tax-exempt, all US citizens must file a tax return annually to the IRS, stating all income earned worldwide. The penalties for non-compliance are very steep. During Karen's next visit to the US she met with a tax accountant, filed amended tax returns and was able to breathe a sigh of relief.

The United States is one of the only countries whose citizens must pay taxes even when they reside elsewhere. However, US citizens will never pay more tax on total income than if it were earned in the US. This can often mean a tax refund for citizens overseas who are already paying tax in countries with a high tax rate. Some countries look beyond annual income and tax overall wealth. The income tax rates of Sweden and Denmark are the highest in Europe at up to 55.9% and 67% respectively. Some African nations have equally high tax tariffs; Senegal and Angola with rates up to 50% and 60%, respectively.

> WATCH OUT!
> **Remember you are ultimately responsible for filing your tax return, do not be passive, be informed.**

Import tax

Duty-free items appeal to travelers because they are 'tax free' but there is a *caveat* often overlooked. Tourists do not have to pay taxes in the purchasing country but people forget they may have to pay import taxes in their home country. Additionally, passengers carry their duty-free purchases onto their flight not realizing the liquid goods have to be added to checked luggage if they take a connecting flight through a country, because of the restrictions related to bringing liquids on a flight.

Import tax may also be charged on novelty items an employee is taking to colleagues or distributing at a convention or trade fair,

> Paul was working in the US and decided to have shirts monogrammed with the company logo for his staff and so he ordered 50 shirts in a range of sizes. When he went to pick them up, US customs advised him he would have to pay import tax on the shirts. The cost was more than the value of the shirts so he did not give the shirts to his team. Some 15 years later he still has a few of those green shirts, which he wears to do garden work.

> TIP
> **Duty and tariffs are commonly charged on merchandise – do your own research ahead of time; it is not always as simple as the sales person would like you to believe.**

QUIZ – THIS IS SO TAXING

1. Match the sales tax rate (rates may be lower for basic items such as food and medicine) and the corresponding country.

Sales Tax Rate	Country
5 %	Liechtenstein
7.6 %	Finland
10%	Japan
13%	New Zealand
15%	Lebanon
23%	Bolivia

2. Who has not been convicted of tax evasion in his/her country?

   a. Actor – Wesley Snipes
   b. German tennis player – Boris Becker
   c. Russian oil tycoon – Mikhail Khodorkovsky
   d. Famous Italian tenor – Luciano Pavarotti
   e. Decorator extraordinaire – Martha Stewart

3. If an American wants to renounce his/her citizenship, for up to how many years of estimated tax may he/she be required to pay, after the request is granted?

   a. 10 years
   b. 7 years
   c. 5 years
   d. 2 years
   e. None

4. The family and life-partner of the author of *The Girl With The Dragon Tattoo* are fighting over inheritance because life-partners are not recognized in the country. In which country is this battle taking place?

   a. Sweden
   b. Norway
   c. Denmark
   d. Finland
   e. Ukraine

5. Put the following country in order of most tax-friendly for corporations.

   _____ Canada
   _____ The Netherlands
   _____ Italy
   _____ Australia
   _____ Mexico

Separation of Church and State

The topic of religion in an intercultural guide might strike some readers as odd and I apologize if this causes offence, however with almost 85% of the world population proclaiming to be members of a religious faith, it cannot be ignored.

Religion is the foundation of many customs, traditions and lives around the world. Although members from diverse religious groups sometimes reside in the same country, religious differences have been the root cause of many of wars and creation of countries. Naturally, the faith of the majority tends to take precedence in an area. The influence of religion is evident in countless areas of life, including:

- Philosophy
- Laws
- Dress
- Holidays

Philosophy

The faithful of every religion have a spectrum within its membership from the very conservative to the very liberal. Employers and schools can face new issues when an employee or student makes a request for religious reasons which is counter to company policy, such as stating they cannot work on Friday evening or requesting time and a place to pray during the work or school day. While fanatics may get press time the majority of believers of any faith want to lead a good life and let others do the same. One of the results of the desire to do good works has been the creation of charitable organizations, consequently many aid groups have a religious connection.

> **TIP**
> Religion is a personal choice – be respectful of people and their rights to believe.

Laws

Challenges can arise in communities when religious and civil laws conflict. Areas where there has been divergence include safety, seeking medical treatment, and dispute resolution. Some governments have enacted laws, which state a face cannot be covered by a veil and parents have been held accountable when they refused life-saving medical treatment for their children in the name of religion. The leaders of a religious group may influence legislation, censorship or have authority in civil disputes. Sometimes members of a faith seek guidance or help with problems from the local religious leader rather than civil authorities.

Some Pakistani immigrants in the United Kingdom prefer to resolve their disputes, including divorce, in compliance with Sharia law. In the UK Sharia is not legally recognized and conflicts with local authorities can arise.

WATCH OUT!
Find out whether religious laws or civil authorities have the last word in your host country.

Weekends and holidays

The five-day working week is becoming more common, although it is not universal. For example in India the workweek is Monday through Saturday. In countries with a five-day working week, the weekends are usually based on the most important day of the religious week, plus one. In the Americas and Europe the day is Sunday and the weekend, Saturday and Sunday. In Israel the Sabbath begins Friday night at sunset and lasts until sunset of Saturday. The Muslim holy day is on Friday so the weekend is Friday and Saturday in most Middle Eastern countries, although a few have chosen Thursday – Friday for their weekend.

The official holidays of a country generally were originally selected based on the important religious days of the predominant religion. After this a few secular days are usually added, such as an independence day, recognition of royalty or a day honoring workers.

> *TIP*
> **Do not assume holidays in one country are the same in another.**

Symbolism

As mentioned in the *Hats Off to You* section, a hat or hairstyle may be a clue to someone's religious affiliation. However, each religion has a plethora of symbols with significance. Some are worn, such as a St. Christopher's medal or Star of David, and others are displayed, such as statues of the virgin Mary in Catholic countries including France, Spain and Malta.

QUIZ – SEPARATION OF CHURCH AND STATE

1. Match the major holiday with the religion:

Holiday	Religion
Easter	Judaism
Yom Kippur	Sikhism
Ramadan	Buddhism
Gurpurbs	Christianity
Vesak	Islam

2. Which country professes the philosophy of 'separation of church and state'?

   a. United Kingdom
   b. Japan
   c. China
   d. United States of America
   e. New Zealand

3. With which religion is the Dalai Lama associated?

   a. Buddhism
   b. Hinduism
   c. Christianity
   d. Islam
   e. Agnosticism

4. A British teacher in Sudan was arrested, jailed and eventually deported for naming a teddy bear?

   a. Mowgli
   b. Muhammad
   c. Yahweh
   d. Hussein

5. Which of the following has a positive impact on local economies?

   a. Food processing (Kosher)
   b. Clothing (Burka, Sari)
   c. Tourism (visiting sights of religious significance – Vatican City, Jerusalem)
   d. Financial dealings (ethics, loaning money)
   e. All of the above

6. Match the symbol and the religion:

Symbol	Religion
Bindi	Catholicism
Rosary	Hindu
Menorah	Greek Orthodox
Byzantine crosses	Buddhism
Eight-spoked wheel	Judaism

CONCLUSION

Wishing You Success

This book has highlighted some of the differences existing between various cultures and I hope it has helped you appreciate what a broad and challenging subject it is. Gaining insight into what and why people do things cannot predict how someone will act/react in a set of circumstances, but it can provide insight into the reasons for a given situation. Successful interactions with other cultures comes from an open mind, knowledge and experience. Good luck in your pursuit of cultural competence; I hope you notice a few more of the subtle differences and don't make too many faux pas.

ANSWERS

THE POWER OF A FEW WORDS

1.

Greeting	Country
Goedemorgen	The Netherlands
Bom dia	Portugal
Bonjour	France
Jó reggelt	Hungary
Ni hao	China

2. d
3. d
4. b
5. b

SPEAKING THE LOCAL LANGUAGE – WHY BOTHER?

1. e
2. b (while the other factors are helpful without practice a person will fail)
3. a

4.

Idiosyncrasy	Language
Capitalizes all nouns	German
No Tenses	Chinese
No gender	Finnish
False Friends*	French

* words that look the same but have different meanings such as 'concierge' in English is the helpful person who arranges theater tickets or dinner reservation in an expensive hotel but in French the word means janitor.

5. e
6. d
7.

Confident		Humble	
Positive	Negative	Positive	Negative
Self-assured	Arrogant	Modest	Insecure
Assured	Conceited	Unassuming	Timid
Self-reliant	Haughty	Retiring	Meek
Sure of yourself	Pompous	Unpretentious	Self-effacing
Proud	Big-headed	Simple	Subservient
Self-sufficient	Cocky	Respectful	Submissive
Stately	Self-important	Without airs	Docile
Regal	Condescending	Plain	Compliant
Imposing	Egotistical	Mild	
Distinguished	Pretentious		
	Boastful		
	Full of oneself		

ENGLISH IS ENGLISH

1. e
2. c
3. d
4.

Word	Country or area of origin
Arsenal	Italy
Giraffe	Arabic
Icon	Russian
Pajamas	Hindi
Tattoo	Pacific Islands

5.

Number of Letters in Alphabet	Language
Forty-six letters	Slovak
Twenty-four letters	Greek
Thirty-three letter	Russian
Eighteen letters	Hawaiian
Twenty-nine letters	Finnish

6. b
7. a. Foot   7 b. Seven

WHAT'S THE WEATHER LIKE BACK HOME?

1.

Safe	Caution	Taboo
Pets	Economy	Personal problems
Films	Accomplishments	Mothers-in-law
Technology	Recent article	Taxes
Community Event		Boss
Trivia		

2. a
3. e
4. b (Individuals from Latin American countries enjoy lively conversation and refuse to let language be a challenge)
5. b (small talk is not unusual at the beginning of a meeting but is rarely used in the middle of a meeting)
6. c
7. a

GETTING THE MESSAGE RIGHT

1. a
2.

Low Context	High Context
Germany	Brazil
The Netherlands	France
USA	Hungary
	Israel
	Russia

3. c
4. a
5.

Low Context	High Context
ASAP	Would you mind
Urgent	Perhaps
Deadline	Appreciated
Now	Please call me

6. d
7. b

THUMBS UP

1. d
2. b (a – can be interpreted as rude in some countries such as Malaysia and offensive in Japan, c – polite in Western Europe and USA, used in Africa, d – used in Philippines)

3.

Gesture	Country (s)
Thumbs up – same as the middle finger in some cultures	Iraq, Afghanistan
Okay - same as the middle finger in some cultures	Mediterranean, Greece
'V' sign (palm inward) – a taunt or challenge, meaning 'F**k off'	United Kingdom
Blow nose loudly – rude, the person should leave the room	Japan
Showing bottom of their feet toward people or Buddha is an insult	Thailand

4.

Approach	Country (s)
Knock on table (one method of applause in meetings)	Germany
Kissing fingers	Latin based countries
Thumbs up (also in USA)	Western Europe
Public recognition is used in many western cultures but not all Eastern ones	United States

5.

Within an elbow's length/ touching	An arm's length/ no touching
Argentina	Bulgaria
Russia	Canada
Spain	Finland
Turkey	The Netherlands
Uzbekistan	United Kingdom

OH, THOSE COLORFUL WORDS WE LEARN

1. c
2. b (usually with sexual connotation)
3.

Less offensive	Offensive words
Shoot	Shit
Darn, dang	Damn
Fudge, fooie, flip	Fuck
Witch	Bitch
Butt	Ass

4. a
5.

Emphasis words	Counterpart
Horrible	Bad
Spectacular	Good
Mundane	Boring
Immaculate	Clean
Fabulous	Fine

DID YOU HEAR THE ONE ABOUT?

1. a
2. b
3.

Humor	Usage
Satire	Political humor
Slapstick	Film
Joke	Stand-up comedy

Cartoon	Newspaper or magazine
Physical antics	Film or television

4.

Definition	Word
Something or someone that makes a person laugh	Funny
Enjoy a activity	Fun
Something that can be tickled by humor	Funny bone
Hearty laugh	Guffaw*
Spoof of a subject	Parody

*Note: other words/phrases with a similar meaning to guffaw are: a belly laugh, to roar with laughter, to crack up

5. d

MAY I HAVE YOUR CARD, PLEASE?

1. d (having a card in the local language is advantageous but if it is not a long-term engagement, the value may not be evident. If the country has multiple national languages as many do; research which language will better serve your needs)

2. a

3. a

4. a

5. b

6. b

MAY I CALL YOU STEVE?

1. c
2. e (*Meneer* is used in the Netherlands and Flanders, *Singh* is used by Sikh men in India, *San* is added to the last name in Japan, *Pan* is used in Poland)
3. c
4. b
5. e
6. c
7. c
8. b (frequently children of foreign parents do not receive automatic citizenship from their country of birth)
9. e

ROUND THE CLOCK

1.

Idiom	Definition
Time is money	Time is very valuable and should always be used productively
Stand the test of time	Something is reliable and not just a trend
Time of your life	Enjoy yourself
A month of Sundays	A long time
Pregnant Pause	A long quiet period usually after a surprising or embarrassing comment

2. c
Explanation:

Country	View of time	Country	View of time
USA	Linear	Mexico	Multi-active
Switzerland	Linear	Italy	Multi-active
Poland	Multi-active	Romania	Multi-active

| Japan | Multi-active | Thailand | Cyclical |
| Finland | Linear | Russia | Multi-active |

3.

Time	Decision making outcome
Linear	Desired tasks accomplished
Multi-active	Made some headway but more work to be done in the following days
Circular	Items discussed, no immediate decisions, some items eventually done others deemed unnecessary

4.

Linear	Multi-active	Circular
Austria	Bolivia	India
New Zealand	Hungary	Thailand
Sweden	Kuwait	Vietnam
USA	Nigeria	

5. b
6. c

SUBSTANCE VS. STYLE

1. c (as mentioned in the humor section entitled 'Did you hear the one about' – a joke is not advisable in a multi-national setting. Note: use vocabulary that matches the language level of the audience to deliver a comprehensible message)
2. e
3. c
4. a
5. b (difficult questions are asked to ensure the idea is factually supported)

ONE SIZE FITS ALL

1. b
2. e
3. a
4. b
5. d

WHERE TO DRAW THE LINE

1. d
2. Giving a gift that is one of the exports of the recipient's country is ill-advised, for example wine in France, Italy or Argentina

Gift	Country
Knife (viewed as desire to server relationship)	Brazil
Clock (produce their own)	Switzerland
Items with large company logos	France
Anything in groups of four	Japan
Caviar (they have easy access to it)	Belarus

3. d
4. a
5. Laws vary by country as to numerous aspects of business conduct. It is easy to know the rules of your own country but imperative to know the ones of the country in which you are conducting business.

ARE YOU HIRING?

1. c (one month for every $20,000 earned, but this was before the financial crisis of 2008)
2. c
3. a
4. b
5. e

ACCOMPANYING PARTNER OR TRAILING SPOUSE?

1. e (partner is not used exclusively for gay couples)

2.

Country	Year
Philippines	Still illegal
Argentina	1530
Ireland	1997
Jordan	1939
United Kingdom	1987

3. e (people are told what they want to hear in order to have a smooth transition)

4.

Idiom	Meaning
A ball and chain	The person is a burden
My better half	The person is an asset, usually a spouse or significant other
Shotgun wedding	Feel obligated to marry due to pregnancy
Marriage (match) made in heaven	The situation is very positive
Footloose and fancy free	No obligations

5. b (the percentage of males accompanying their spouse is very small, around 10 %)

DO THE NUMBERS ADD UP?

1. The date will be different for each reader but remember the formats:
   United States = mmddyyyy,
   Europe = ddmmyyyy
   Japan = yyyymmdd

2. Match the international country calling code and their corresponding country:

Calling codes	Country
30	Greece
254	Kenya
51	Peru
60	Malaysia
354	Iceland

3. d
4.

Zip/Postal codes	Country
200040	China
1016 GZ	The Netherlands
2609	Australia
SW1X 7RN	England
None used	Qatar

5.

Idiom	Meaning
Count your lucky stars	Recognize the positive aspects of life
Take five	Take a break

Someone's days are numbered	Very little time is left in a situation (e.g. might be laid-off)
Don't count your chickens before they hatch	Raise your expectations too soon and disappointment may occur
The person is on cloud nine	Very happy

THE DEVIL'S IN THE DETAILS

1. b (DVDs are coded into six regions)

2. a (the US and Canada)

3. d

4. b (there are approximately 13 major types of AC plugs)

5. b

6.

Queen-size bed dimensions	Country
60x80 inches (152x203 cm)	Brazil
60x80 inches (152x203 cm)	Australia
63x79 inches (160x200 cm)	Europe
60x77 inches (152x196 cm)	Japan

MAY I HELP YOU?

1.

Company	Slogan
Coca Cola	It's the Real Thing (1971)
Mercedes Benz	The Best or Nothing (2010)
Sony	Make Believe (2009)
Nike	Just Do It
De Beers Consolidated Mines	Diamonds are Forever

2. a

3.

Positive	Negative
Inexpensive	Cheap
Bargain	Slick
Smooth	Quibble
Expensive	Pricey
High-end	Haggle
Sincere	
Polished	
Negotiate	

4.

Idiom	Meaning
A lemon	Poor quality product, usually an automobile
Beat Around the Bush	Avoid answering question or concern
A Diamond in the Rough	Something or person with potential, but needs a bit of work.
Give Someone a Rain Check	Agree to do something at a later date, (originally stores gave customers a rain check when a sale item was sold out – the customer could return to buy the item at the same low price)

A pigeon	A naïve person who can easily be cheated
Fine print	Important terms of an agreement which usually favor the seller over the buyer
Caveat Emptor (Latin)	Let the buyer beware

5.

Material	Damage
Metal/aluminum	Dent
Porcelain/China/Pottery	Crack, shatter
Leather	Scuff
Clothing	Tear, snag
Silver, Bronze	Tarnish

DOMESTIC GODDESS

1. a
2. a
3.

Hand-wash   No bleach   Tumble dry   Iron on medium   Dry clean

© copyright symbols by Ginetex

4. d
5. c
6. a

BUT IT WAS ON TELEVISION

1. b
2. a
3. c
4. b (a 'trust fund' suggests plenty of money, while a savings account simply means an indeterminate amount of money)
5.

Modification method	Country
Brazil	Dubbing using Brazilian Portuguese
Croatia	Subtitles
Greece	Subtitles
Israel	Subtitles in Hebrew and Russian
Ukraine	Dubbing

ONE STOP SHOPPING

1.

Fruit and Vegetable	Country
Orange	Brazil
Apples	China
Olive	Spain
Pea	Canada
Cacao Bean	Côte d'Ivoire aka Ivory Coast

2. a
3. d

4.

Food Group	Specialty shop
Pastries	Bakery
Poultry, veal, sausage	Butcher shop
Fresh produce	Farmers market
Corn beef, gouda, gorgonzola	Deli
Wheat germ, organic products	Health food store

5. c
6. b

THE GRAMMAR OF FOOD

1.

Doughnut name	Country
Smoutebollen	Belgium
Sufganiyot	Israel
Kreppel/Krapfen	Germany
Lihapiirakka	Finland

2.

United Kingdom	United States
Banger	Sausage
Fairy cake	Cup cake
Jelly	Jell-O (gelatin dessert)
Minced meat	Ground beef
Pudding	Dessert

3. d
4. a
5. a
6.

Chocolate manufacturer	Country
Nestlé	Switzerland
Neuhaus	Belgium
Ferrero	Italy
Hershey	United States
El Rey	Venezuela

IT'S A CELEBRATION!

1.

Country	Public Holidays
Egypt	16 days
Chile	18 days
Bosnia	27 days
Saudi Arabia	21 days
Russia	12 days

2. a

3.

Country	Food Item
United Kingdom	Christmas pudding
Germany	Knoedel
Switzerland	Cheese fondue
India	Vindaloo sauce
Japan	Osechi-ryori

4. d
5. c
6. b

POLITE OR RUDE? THAT IS THE QUESTION.

1. c
2. e
3. b (a person should wait for the host/hostess or permission from the others at the table)
4. c
5.

Leaving food on your plate is fine/good	Leaving food on your plate is negative
India	Greece
Russia	Korea
South Africa	Mexico
USA	Sweden
	Turkey
	Vietnam

6. b
7.

Place of Honor	Country
Away from the door	Japan
To the right of the host	United States
At the end of the table	Romania
Middle of the table	Greece

CHEERS!

1.

Toast	Country
Zum Wohl	Germany
Saude	Brazil
Ganbei	China
Salud	Spain
Stolat	Poland

2. c
3. b
4.

Toasting custom	Country
Drink only after the first toast is offered	Russia
The glass is emptied, the last few drops are shaken out, then the host refills the glass	Korea
Make eye contact with every person you are toasting	Sweden
The guest of honor is toasted and should reciprocate	USA
Toasting is rarely done	Middle East

5. a
6. a
7. c

BABIES, WEDDINGS, FUNERALS

1. c
2.

Message	Country
Put at grave site on November 1st	Belgium
Used to create corsages particularly for school events	United States
Royal flower, given on special occasions	Japan

3. Payment responsibility may fall to the employer, the country or some combination and is not necessarily 100%. (Other countries may also fall into the same category)

Parental Paid Days	Countries
Zero	United States, Swaziland
90 days	China, Korea, Thailand
12 weeks	Mexico, Ghana, Nigeria
18 weeks	Chile, Cuba
More than 1 year	Germany, Norway, Sweden

4. a
5.

Wedding custom	Country
Bride wears hues of red	India
Separate receptions for men and women	UAE
Wedding cake is a fruitcake	Scotland
Wedding rings worn on right hand	Europe
Women only wore tops after marriage	Zulu tribe in South Africa

6. c

7. d (a & b - beliefs held by Jewish followers and various western European nationals; c – concerns of Vietnamese and e – many Russians)

HATS OFF TO YOU

1. c
2.

Idiom	Meaning
Throw one's hat in the ring	Indicate interest in something
Hats off to you	Indicates admiration for someone
At the drop of a hat	Very quickly
A bee in their bonnet	Annoyed
To be head to head	Equal

3. c
4.

Headwear	Explanation
Stetson	Another name for a Cowboy hat
Songkok	Indonesia, Brunei, Malaysia, Singapore, the southern Philippines and southern Thailand,
Stocking cap	Worn skiing
Kufi	Originates from Africa
Beret	Worn by some military & French

5. a

6. b (ultra conservative Orthodox Jewish women, after marriage and from then on they wear a wig)

NAKED OR NUDE?

1. c & d (an exhibitionist is classified as a sexual deviant who exposes himself to unsuspecting passersby; a streaker is male or female who runs through a public area or event for shock value)
2. d
3. a
4. c
5. b
6. e

LUCK OF THE IRISH

1. a

2. d (cricket – good luck in China and for native Americans, horse shoe - Greeks and Christians but it needs to face upward to hold the luck, Chimney sweep – brings good luck when seen in Germany, Elephant – in Feng Shui and Hindu)

3. e (a – knives are interpreted as a desire to sever the relationship in Brazil & Argentina; b & c – a broke mirror brings seven years of bad luck and a black cat passing your path is not positive in the opinion of Americans; d – bathing and/or showering will bring bad luck is a belief held by some Chinese.

4.

Country	Good luck
Germany	Pig
Ireland	Shamrock
China	Red Envelope
Italy	Fish
India	Sapphire

5. a

6.

National flower	Country
Lotus	Egypt
Daffodil	Wales
A blue water lily - Nil Manel	Sri Lanka
An orchid - guaria morada	Costa Rica
Black Iris	Jordan

MAN'S BEST FRIEND

1. b
2. a
3. e
4. b
5. c

THIS IS SO TAXING

1.

Sales Tax Rate	Country
7.6 %	Liechtenstein
23 %	Finland
5%	Japan
15%	New Zealand
10%	Lebanon
13%	Bolivia

2. d
3. a

4. a

5. Most tax-friendly countries:

1) Mexico
2) Canada
3) The Netherlands
4) Australia
5) Italy

SEPARATION OF CHURCH AND STATE

1.

Holiday	Religion
Easter	Christianity
Yom Kippur	Judaism
Ramadan	Islam
Gurpurbs	Sikhism
Vesak	Buddhism

2. d

3. a

4. b

5. e (their revenues are driven markedly by religion)

6. Match the symbol and the religion:

Symbol	Religion
Bindi	Hindu
Rosary	Catholicism
Menorah	Judaism
Byzantine crosses	Greek Orthodox
Eight-spoked wheel	Buddhism

RESOURCES

Books

A Moveable Marriage; Relocate Your Relationship without Breaking It, Robin Pascoe, Expatriate Press Limited (2005)

Cultural Intelligence - A Guide to Working With People From Other Cultures, Brooks Peterson, Intercultural Press Inc. (2004)

Doing Business in Brazil, video with Dean Foster, http://www.youtube.com/watch?v=EwWyFGnHFS0&feature=related, January 5, 2011

Expat Women: Confessions - 50 Answers to Your Real-Life Questions About Living Abroad, Andrea Martins and Victoria Hepworth, Expat Women Enterprises Pty LTD ATF Expat Women Trust (2011)

Intercultural Business Communication, Robert Gibson Oxford University Press (2002)

Kiss, Bow, or Shake Hands (2nd Edition), Terri Morison and Wayne A. Conaway, Adams Media (2006)

Louder Than words... Nonverbal Communication, Mele Koneya and Alton Barbour, Published by Merrill (1976)

Mind Your Manners: Managing Business Cultures in The New Global Europe (3rd Edition), John Mole, Nicholas Brealey Publishing (2011)

Multicultural Manners: Essential Rules of Etiquette for the 21st Century, Norine Dresser, John Wiley and Sons, Inc. (2005)

Rules, Britannia: An insider's Guide to Life in the United Kingdom, Toni Summers Hargis, St. Martin's Press (2006)

Sixty Million Frenchmen Can't Be Wrong: Why We love France But Not The French, Jean Benoît and Julie Barlow, Sourcebooks, Inc. (2003)

The Global Nomad's Guide to University Transition, Tina L. Quick, Summertime Publishing (2010)

The Hints Book: Living and Working in Belgium (19th Edition), Nancy Kapstein and Meredith Spangenberg, American Women's Club of Brussels (2007)

The Unofficial Guide to Having a Baby, by Ann Douglas and John R. Sussman, MD, John Wiley and Sons (2004)

When Cultures Collide: Leading Across Cultures (3rd Edition), Richard D. Lewis, Nicholas Brealey Publishing (2009)

When in Rome or Rio or Riyadh…: Cultural Q&A for Successful Business Behavior Around the World, Gwyneth Olofsson, International Press (2004)

Articles

11 Tips for Working with Americans, Allyson Stewart Allen, www.workingwithamericans.com , November 11, 2011

285 Indian Girls Shed 'Unwanted Names', source: Associated Press, www.usatoday.com, October 22, 2011

After Early Errors, Wal-Mart Thinks Locally To Act Globally, Miguel Bustillo, http://online.wsj.com, August 14, 2009

Alcatel-Lucent Confronts Its Cross-cultural Challenges, www.leaderswedeserve.wordpress.com, posted July 31, 2008

Building Resilience for 2012, Ruth Forsythe, Intercultural Blogs, www.worldpress.com

Can Africa Keep Time ?, BBC News, www.bbc.co.uk October 28, 2003

Canada Funds College To Provide Programs For Immigrants, www.workpermit.com, May 19, 2008

Canada Helps Immigrants Achieve Success, www.workpermit.com, March 23, 2008

Canadian Citizenship Language Requirements Change, www.workpermit.com, October 28, 2011

Changing Demographics of US Science – Engineering PhDs, by David R. Francis, www.nber.org January 2005

Coca-Cola Chief Muhtar Kent Is Lost in Translation Toasting Hu in Japanese, by Michael Forsythe, www.bloomberg.com January 20, 2011

Cross-cultural Branding and Leadership, Martin Roll, www.venturerepublic.com

Cultural Sensitivity in Business, by Neil Payne, Kwintessential Ltd

Culture Clash Hits Home at Alcatel-Lucent, Kevin J O'Brien contributing from Berlin and Laura Holson contributing from New York, The New York Times, July 29, 2008

Disney Opens Itself To Cultural Difference And Adapts Its Latest Park To The Local Culture, Caroline Goutard, www.marketing-planet.com, September 15, 2005

Do Learning Styles Change As We Get Older?, Kate Hagen, http://kateahagen.wordpress.com, July 7, 2009

Doing Business in USA, www.todaytranslations.com, November 11, 2011

EuroDisney, Manfred F. R. Kets, Chief Executive Publishing (1994)

Flower Etiquette, www.advancedetiquette.com, May 19, 2011

Foreign Firms Expanding To US Face Uphill Battle, premium content from Atlanta Business Chronicle by Randy Southerland, contributing writer, www.bizjournals.com, November 4, 2011

Hong Kong Disneyland Feng Shui Secrets and Facts, http://www.disneylandreport.com, (2006)

How An Overseas Job Can Affect Family Life, Kim Gittleson, www.bbc.co.uk/news/business, December 15, 2011

How Long Does It Take to Find A New Job? Perri Capell, http://.online.wjs.com, April 28, 2008

Japanese Non-verbal Communication, http://students.ed.uiuc.edu

McDonald's, www.spritus-temporis.com/mcdonald-s/challenges, January 14, 2011

Merkel Says German Multi-Cultural Society Has Failed, Audrey Kauffmann, http://new.yahoo.com, October 17, 2010

M.I.A. Flips Bird During Super Bowl Halftime Show, David Bauder, Associated Press http://news.yahoo.com, February 6, 2012

Module 3 – The Intercultural Challenge: Doing Business Globally, www.worldwideerc.org, downloaded July 2011

More American Expatriates Give Up Citizenship, Brian Knowlton, www.nytimes.com, April 25, 2010

Nike and 9/11, Daniel Pipes New York Sun, September 12, 2006

Novel Insights Into The Foundering Daimler-Chrysler Merger: Report of remarks made by Peter Schneider, http://knowledge.emory.edu, (June 5, 2002)

Siemens' Culture Clash; CEO Kleinfeld Is Making Changes, And Enemies – Including Within The Ranks, Jack Ewing, Business Week, January 29, 2007

Studios Try To Lessen What's Lost in Translation, Glenn Whipp for The Associated Press, www.yahoo.com, July 18, 2011

Survivor Lauren Manning Finds 'New Normal' After 9/11, Bob Minzesheimer, www.usatoday.com, August 29, 2011

Tesco's Stumble into the US Market, Sean Silverthorne, Harvard Business School (HBS) Working Knowledge, October 25, 2010

The Failure of Retail Internationalisation in Marks and Spencer, Steve Burt, European Retail Digest, September 1, 2002

The Six Elements of an Effective Presentations, Tony Luna, www.photo.net, July 2009

Understanding the Narrative in Workplace Relationships, by Diversity in Motion, October 27, 2011

Wal-Mart Finds That Its Formula Doesn't Fit Every Culture, Mark Landler and Michael Barbaro, The New York Times, August 2, 2006

Wal-Mart Selling Stores and Leaving South Korea, Choe Sang-Hun, International Herald Tribune, May 23, 2006

Why Wal-Mart Can't Find Happiness In Japan, William J. Holstein, www.CNN Money.com July 27, 2007

Who Gets The Most (The Least) Vacation, Jeanne Sahadi, http://cnnmoney.com, June 14, 2007

Websites

http://www.kwintessential.co.uk – country specific information

www.culturecrossing.net – country specific information

www.etiquettescholar.com – country specific information

www.worldbank.org – country statistics

http://www.tjc-oxford.com – country specific information

nl.wikipedia.org/wiki/Lijst van landen naar BNP met sectoraandelen - country statistics

Numerous government websites

Other Resources

ELAN: Effects on the European Economy of Shortages of Foreign Language Skills in Enterprise, European Commission (2005)

Perfect Presentations: How You Can Master the Art of Success Presenting, Andrew Ivey, Ventus Publishing ApS (2010)

The Feedback Message: Reconciling Communication Styles Across Cultures, Presentation by David Trickey, TCO International Diversity Management (2010)

The Impact of Culture on M&A: Doing Something About It, Mercer Ltd (2009)

ABOUT THE AUTHOR

Elizabeth Vennekens-Kelly is an intercultural trainer and consultant. She was born and raised in the United States. Elizabeth was a business executive in the United States for twenty years before relocating to Europe. She has spent the last 10 years working in Western Europe, interacting with individuals from more than 40 countries around the world, professionally and personally, where she has gained invaluable knowledge about individual cultures. Elizabeth has combined her business experience, familiarity of expat living and intercultural knowledge to help those relocating and doing business overseas to effectively interact and communicate in multi-cultural situations. Elizabeth works with both individuals and groups, conducts training seminars, workshops and gives intercultural presentations throughout Europe. She has worked with people from numerous firms, organizations and companies such as Sony, Honeywell, European Central Bank, Suez Energy, Janssen Pharmaceutica, and Bloomberg Financial.

Her philosophy is: *Good management and communication skills are essential to effective business leaders, similarly having cultural competencies are vital to effective managers working in multi-national companies.*

Management and communication skills, along with intercultural interactions are not complex concepts, but when they are not understood and utilized, the results can be very costly.

Elizabeth is a member of organizations including SIETAR, FIGT, AWCA, MIWC and FAWCO. She served as the Chairperson of FAWCO's Sharing Cultures Task Force (2009-2013).

Her goal is to help individuals develop the cultural competencies they need to be successful and to encourage people to make the most of the unique opportunity of living outside their passport country.

In addition to English, Elizabeth speaks Dutch and has a working knowledge of German.

CPSIA information can be obtained at www.ICGtesting.com
Printed in the USA
BVOW10s1852180115

383745BV00006B/127/P